"Kristen captures the powerful forces at play in inheritance. More importantly, she shows us how people harness those forces to live happy and productive lives. She does this by telling an emotionally honest story of how a family came to align their wealth with their values and gain the wisdom to create a lasting legacy beyond the mere preservation of financial wealth. In telling this story, she combines deep insight with warmth, acceptance, and understanding. In that sense, this book not only brings insight and intelligence to a very complex experience but it also reflects the care and compassion so necessary to traverse these difficult transitions. For anyone who is passing on wealth or who will receive it, I recommend that you pick up and read this small gem of genuine wisdom."

Matthew Wesley, Wealth Advisor

"The questions at the end of each chapter artfully prompt insightful thought from the reader—a perfect learning tool for families and advisors."

Karen Calcagno, *PCC*, Founder and Legacy Coach at Advantage Family Business Center

"An old story about family wealth told in a new and refreshing way. A must read. If you are a financially successful family, or a Trusted Advisor, this must be one of the books on your shelf."

Richard Orlando, CEO of Legacy Capitals and author of *Legacy: The Hidden Keys to Optimizing Your Family Wealth Decisions*

in THREE GENERATIONS

Live Your Legacy!

Kurt T Hey

in THREE GENERATIONS

A Story About Family, Wealth,
and Beating the Odds

Kristen Heaney, MSW, BCC

In Three Generations:
A Story About Family, Wealth, and Beating the Odds
Published by Blue Tide Press
Vero Beach, FL

Library of Congress Control Number: 2017938450
ISBN: 978-0-9987537-0-6

BUSINESS & ECONOMICS / Finance / Wealth Management

QUANTITY PURCHASES: Schools, companies, professional
groups, clubs, and other organizations may qualify for special
terms when ordering quantities of this title. For information,
email info@BlueTidePress.com

BLUE TIDE
P R E S S

to OKT, LDH, and KLH
your legacy lives on

Acknowledgments

I offer my sincere gratitude to the professionals in the field who have taught me so much and influenced my life, work, and writing in direct and indirect ways: Richard Orlando, Hartley Goldstone, Matthew Wesley, Jim Grubman, John A. Warnick, Nathan Dungan, Dennis Jaffe, Jay Hughes, Roy Williams, and Vic Preisser.

To Miyagi: Thank you for taking a chance on me, for the confidence you instill, and for all the wisdom you so generously share.

To my Brother: Your edits brought great depth to this story, and made it so much more meaningful. I'm so grateful for your support and encouragement.

To Ryan: Thank you for teaching me to love, and for your unwavering dedication to me, our family and the legacy we're carrying together. You and I are a great team. I'm so proud of us.

To my next generation: Life with you brings me so much joy and makes me want to be a better person each day. You are truly exceptional people, and I'm so lucky I get to be your mom.

To the God of the universe, who always has me on some grand adventure of spiritual growth: I continue to dedicate all I have to You for Your purposes in this world and the next. Please keep guiding my path.

A Note to the Reader

Thank you for choosing to read this book. In a world with so many beautifully written words to read, I feel grateful that you have taken the time to read mine.

I chose to write this story in a unique "truth wrapped in story" style because I have been moved and inspired by several parable-style leadership stories, including the works of Patrick Lencioni, the Arbinger Institute, Og Mandino, and of course, Jesus Christ as recorded in the Bible. There's something about looking at a fictional character's life from the outside in that helps us see the course of our own lives in a new light. I wanted to bring a relatable story to the field of wealth legacy, but I also wanted to offer readers some practical strategies to apply to their own lives. This story isn't just about the Hannigans; it's about all of us. Regardless of our financial status, money plays a significant role in our lives and can mess with our values, identity, and relationships. For families with substantial wealth, the risks of these challenges are even greater.

As both a wealth legacy coach and a second-generation inheritor, I have great passion for both wealthy families and the advisors who serve them. The wealthy are a uniquely misunderstood group. The struggles of affluence are lonely struggles, clouded by a great void of conversation, and I hope that this story will help to bring a new language of connection to all those who lie awake at night, their minds cluttered with concerns that have historically had no place for discussion amongst friends.

I had main two concerns while writing this book. First, I didn't want it to come across as preachy: "You should be doing this." "You're doing it all wrong." "If you just did it this way, life would be easy." Yuck. I believe that we all have our own journey to walk, our own 'sacred serendipity,' and our own important timing to the course of our growth trajectory. There's nothing worse than a book that leaves you feeling bad about yourself and overwhelmed with a long list of changes you feel pressured to make. I hope that Lane Brock, the legacy coach in the story, will become the encouraging—but never critical—British-accented voice in your head (as she has for me), with her thoughtful questions inspiring you to define your legacy and live it out more strategically. My dream is that this story will become a launching point for you to get involved with a legacy coach or take a self-growth journey with one of the many outstanding nonfiction books on the topic of legacy. The multifaceted legacy of your life is simply too valuable to let its impact die with you.

Secondly, because the idea for this book was inspired by my own story, I worried with every word I wrote that readers would assume commonalities between the characters in the book and my own family members. The characters in this book are vivid and real to me, but completely distinct from any person I've ever met. Campbell and Cole came to life as I read countless nonfiction books, watched documentaries, poured over research, listened to experienced advisors, and sat across from my own clients facing the triumphs and tragedies of wealth. The characters in this story are a bit of you and me and everyone we've ever met. They are the doctor, the tech investor, the lottery winner, the farmer, the NFL player, the overnight celebrity, the inheritor, and the unexpected millionaire next door.

So let me be clear, this story is not my own life story. It is inspired by the experience of losing my father and inheriting wealth at a young age, but any similarity between the characters in this story and those in my own life is purely coincidental and unintentional. Unlike Cole, my own brother has led our family business with wisdom and success, and is a stable, involved father whom I admire and respect. Unlike Debbie, my own mother is compassionate, thoughtful, and one of the most loving people I have ever met. And I can only hope to have the wise moxie under pressure and dedication to her family that Campbell displays throughout the story. In most ways, Jim and my dad are two very different people, but I did rely heavily on my own experience with my father for setting and tone, mostly because it brought back some beautiful memories of him.

Sure, the story would have been more distinct from my own if I had not placed the setting in Detroit (where I grew up), but I really wanted to honor my hometown, and the words just didn't seem to fit in any other location. Detroit is a unique place, full of hardworking, down-to-earth people. To the outside world, the legacy of Detroit is tarnished and hopeless. To Detroiters, the story isn't over yet. Detroiters are realists. We are fighters. If we can handle cold, gray days for six months of every year and roads speckled with tire-sized potholes, we can handle just about anything you throw at us. Thank you for all that you have built in me, Detroit. Your legacy lives inside me. I may have bailed on you for a warmer, sunnier climate, but this story is my homage to you.

No matter who you are, I hope this story finds you at just the right time. If you are a trusted advisor to wealthy families, I hope this book will help you understand and serve your clients in such a way that you will one day look back on your professional career and know that you made a positive impact on generations of client families. If you are a member of a family with substantial wealth, I hope this story is a catalyst for you to consider and discuss the often overwhelming and emotional challenges of family wealth and family legacy. Grab a friend, hire a coach, participate in an online coaching group at my website. This accountability will help you power through the questions at the end of each chapter and apply the Hannigan story to your own life. More than anything, I hope this story makes you hell bent on living in a way that ensures that beneficial legacy of your life will still be shining strong in three generations.

Songs to Inspire Legacy

I thought I'd share my writing playlist, a compilation of songs that got me thinking about my legacy and the legacy of those who have gone before me. This list is by no means exhaustive, so I invite you to email me your favorites and I'll post your updates on www.inthreegenerations.com!

"The Journey of Your Life," Jake Owen
"This is Your Life," Switchfoot
"Now and Forever," Carole King
"100 Years," Five for Fighting
"Humble and Kind," Tim McGraw
"Day That Never Ends," Re:Zound
"The Best Day," Taylor Swift
"Life Is Beautiful," The Afters
"Hold On to What You Believe," Mumford & Sons
"My Own Two Hands," Ben Harper and Jack Johnson
"Make Something Beautiful," Ben Rector
"I'm Alive," Kenny Chesney (featuring Dave Matthews)
"Roots," Parmalee
"Don't Blink," Kenny Chesney
"Slow Down," Nichole Nordeman
"You're Not There," Lukas Graham
"What Matters Most," Barbara Streisand
"My Old Man's Son," Eli Young Band
"Hundred More Years," Francesca Battistelli
"My Boy," Neil Young
"Mercy," Dave Matthews Band

Timeline

1993

That One Dreaded Chapter

Sometimes life just seems like chapters.
Some good, some bad, but all come together
to create the story of our lives.
—Anonymous

Every life story has that one dreaded chapter where it all falls apart. A racing heartbeat drowns out the sound of the outside world.

Boom—Boom—Boom.

All that once was solid slips like sand through desperate, grasping fingers.

Campbell's chapter began with a phone call. Played out like a clichéd scene in a movie, the telephone rang a cacophonous irony into the room as her young voice answered excitedly.

"Hello?"

"Campbell, it's Cole. I...Um...Uh...I have some bad news," shared her older brother, skipping the normal niceties. Campbell's mouth became dry and her chest tightened.

"Cole? What is it?"

"It's Dad. We're at the ER. He's had some numbness in his chin for the past few weeks, but he didn't think it was anything serious, so they sent him to the dentist, which turned out to be a huge waste of time. We didn't want to worry you while you were away at college. Dad said he wanted you to focus on school…" he rambled on, tripping over his words.

"Cole, WHAT?" Campbell insisted.

"He had a CT scan today that showed brain cancer. Dad has brain cancer. It's really bad, Campbell. The doctors say it's terminal, so we think you should come home."

"No," Campbell whispered, putting her hand to her forehead, trying to process what she was hearing. A cold sweat broke out on the back of her neck, underneath her long red hair, as she tried desperately to pull together a reply. "Okay, I'll be home as soon as I can."

As the phone call ended, her mind went into overdrive. Anyone whose life story contains a similar chapter knows that along with intense emotional bad news comes an unexpected ability to plan, organize, and behave remarkably stoically. This protective "go mode" allowed Campbell to make arrangements for the flight back to Detroit that evening, email professors about her absence, and pack appropriate clothing (including funeral clothes, just in case).

Within hours that seemed like minutes, she was boarding a flight to the Midwest. Her eyes darted about, seeking seat B20. Her tall, thin frame settled into the middle seat; she slid her backpack under the cramped space in front of her. With nothing but time until the airplane landed, she leaned her head back and carefully allowed reality to sink into her heart and mind.

"How can this be happening?" she asked herself. "I'm twenty-one years old. How can my dad be dying?"

Her mind drifted back over her childhood years. Her parents, who divorced when she was in middle school, had raised her and her brother in the "sweet spot."

The sweet spot is that place where a family has enough money to protect them from many of life's problems but not enough money to create many of life's problems. Living in the sweet spot meant Campbell's family always had what they needed (and even some of what they wanted), and that money rarely even came up in conversation because it was neither scarce nor superfluous.

In order to arrive at this sweet spot, there had been some sacrifice, of course. Campbell's father, Jim, had invested long hours and a great deal of stress growing his business, which kept him distant in her early childhood years.

What Campbell didn't know is that her perception of her father's financial means was skewed. While Jim had chosen to live life as a sweet-spot family, his bank statements indicated far greater wealth, accrued so quickly in the booming 80s that he hadn't had time to adjust his lifestyle. He figured his kids were better off not knowing anyway.

"He worked so hard all his life and now he won't even get to enjoy it," she thought as a tear ran down her cheek. She closed her eyes and listened to the rhythm of quiet snores coming from the old man propped up against the window in the seat next to her. The rhythm of his breath somehow brought a calming assurance to her racing mind.

She thought of all the family moments spent each Sunday at her grandparents' house. This ritual marked the one time during the week when they were all together, when she had full access to her father. During the hour's drive to and from her grandparents' country home, she reveled in the chance to be with her often-absent father.

She tried desperately to recall the smell of combined cigarette smoke and Halston cologne that filled the car on those Sundays. The Sunday sounds flooded her memory as well, like her father's annoying and adorable habit of playing the same country song—the song of the month, he called it—over and over again until she begged him to stop. The sight of his hands—strong, freckled, and fair—danced in her mind. Hands that were not yet marked with spots of age or wear. They were giant, happy hands that brought her such comfort as a child when she was scared or lonely. Now it would be her holding his hand, bringing him comfort, and this meant that absolutely everything had changed.

Terminal. Cancer.

As the miles flew by underneath her dark airplane window, it was as if her grief had already begun.

YOUR TIME TO REFLECT

Campbell was raised in the sweet spot, protected from the awareness of the degree of her family's wealth, but never without basic needs and a handful of wants met. Some families with wealth raise their children completely unaware of their financial means, while others choose to raise their children with a full understanding of their financial means.

1. How did your family handle passing down knowledge of your family's financial means?

2. What actions or behaviors occur in wealthy families that communicate, in indirect or nonverbal ways, the extent of the family's wealth?

3. What problems do you think might arise out of Campbell's lack of awareness about the extent of her father's wealth as they face his death?

4. What do you think is the healthiest way for wealthy families to communicate to their children about the extent of their wealth?

5. Is there a certain age by which children should be told the whole story? What are the benefits and risks of full disclosure?

1993

Hand of Cards

We cannot change the cards we are dealt,
just how we play the hand.
— *Randy Pausch,* The Last Lecture

Staring death squarely in its steely cold eyes brings an intense, bittersweet beauty to every moment, every conversation shared with a loved one, every glimpse of the rising sun, every smile that brightens the face of your children, and even every tear shed together.

As Jim reflected on his terminal diagnosis, he knew it had changed him, that it had changed everything. He sat sideways on the upholstered window seat of his ninth-floor hospital room, arms crossed, gazing down upon the dirty streets and worn buildings of Detroit. The scene brought to mind a moment he'd shared with his youngest child, Campbell, when she was just a young girl. Reveling in every second of her first airplane ride, she looked out the tiny window, down upon the streets of Detroit, and announced to him (and the three surrounding rows of passengers), "Daddy, Daddy, look! Downtown Detroit looks just radiant from up here!"

Leave it to Campbell to find the rare beauty in one of the country's most forsaken cities.

Somehow now, in light of the events of the last two days, he had a better grasp on the beauty she could see that night. This cancer, this death sentence, had left him grasping for more. Grasping for moments. It had made him desperate to feel more fully alive. He thought of the times he had enjoyed a baseball game at the city's iconic Tiger Stadium. He remembered fondly the dates he had taken to dine with him at the historic Whitney. He reflected upon the meals he'd shared with his kids at Detroit's famous Greektown restaurants. Jim wished for more of those moments, but he was almost out of time. He was gaining a new perspective on his life, a perspective that brought an eye-opening beauty to everything that was once so ordinary. He saw his own life from the proverbial airplane window, and surprisingly, he could see everything so much more clearly.

Things that once seemed to be the most important were now inconsequential. No one bargains with the Grim Reaper for more time to make one more sale or write one more report. In fact, Jim, like most terminal patients, looked back at his life and wished he hadn't worked so hard.

Sure, Jim was pleased he would leave his children in a very healthy financial position, but it seemed he was just getting started doing the important things. Something about death helped him see the beauty of his life with such clarity, but it also brought with it a deep, dull pain that clutched his heart.

He turned away from the window to lie down in a hospital bed that felt littered with regrets. There was so much he had wanted to teach his kids, especially his daughter, Campbell, hopelessly right-brained, about how to handle the substantial wealth she would inherit after his passing. For heaven's sake, she didn't even pay her own telephone bill! This was a job he'd asked his assistant, Cynthia, to do for his daughter, thinking it would be one less task to distract her from her college studies. Damn stubborn girl wouldn't even agree to take an econ class in college.

Jim glanced quickly at the door and stole another long sip from the flask of highbrow scotch that he had smuggled into the hospital, knowing he would need liquid courage to face the doctors' diagnosis.

Maybe he had done it all wrong, protecting the kids from knowing how much wealth they'd inherit at his death. All those times he had asked them to sign the bottom of legal documents, covering the rest of the page to hide figures from their view, so they wouldn't know how much money they had in waiting. He didn't want it to ruin them. Campbell: a sweet, beautiful, passionate girl with a good heart. Cole: a smart, focused, conscientious kid with a solid work ethic. Jim assumed he'd have more time to reveal the full picture to his kids, but now he regretted having to hand such a heavy load to them at his hospital bedside. There simply wasn't time to prepare them for all they would need to know.

He thought of Cole. He was just a kid in his mid-twenties; how could he be successful in taking over Jim's automotive supply business? What respect would the employees and customers give him? How would he manage all the pressure? Jim had hoped to walk Cole through a slow and deliberate succession plan. None of this was happening how he had expected.

Knowing all that Jim needed to accomplish in the short time that remained, Cynthia, his top-notch executive assistant, had researched and hired a consultant to help him. There were legal papers to draft and sign, conversations that needed to take place, a business succession plan to carry out, and so much more. Jim looked at his watch and opened the side-table drawer to hide the evidence of his favorite coping skill, the reliable friend in a bottle that never judged and always helped put his racing mind at ease.

Right on time, a smartly-dressed woman in her late forties with poker-straight brown hair that just barely touched the shoulders of her perfectly-tailored, navy-blue suit appeared in the hospital room doorway and walked to Jim's bedside, reaching out her hand. Her thin hands were cold from the brisk hospital air.

"Good evening, Mr. Hannigan. Lane Brock, wealth legacy consultant. I'm pleased to meet you but terribly sorry to hear of your diagnosis."

"Hello, and please, call me Jim."

Jim was a man who rarely felt unsure of himself. He was well-respected for his hard work, success, and integrity. As a result, he was confident in most settings. From his small, squeaky hospital bed, however, Jim felt small and self-conscious meeting Lane Brock, the foremost expert in her field, with her striking green eyes and British accent.

"Thank you, Jim. Are you feeling well enough at the moment to begin our work together?"

"Yes, I'm anxious to get started. Sounds like I can't be sure when I'll start to lose power up top," he said with a quick side smile, pointing to his head. "So let's get working while I've still got all my marbles."

"It's good to see your sense of humor remains intact. I've already met with your assistant, Cynthia, to gather the details of your business, a rough financial snapshot, and any prior estate-planning documents. However, before we get into all of those details, I'd like to slow down a bit. You've just experienced something very difficult. I want to begin by asking, how are you handling your diagnosis of terminal cancer?"

Everyone asks a dying man, "How are you?" usually delivered with fear, pity, and an unspoken plea for some positive, reassuring answer: "I'm hanging in there," "As good as can be expected," or "It was a hard blow, but we're doing the best we can."

Lane asked the same question, but the way she communicated it told him that she expected candor and was fully capable of handling it.

"It's, uhhhh..." He struggled to find the words to express the harrowing experience of facing his own death. Jim was never very good at talking about feelings, but he couldn't hold back the relentless waves of fear and uncertainty he felt. "This is pretty scary stuff, you know. You worry about your body breaking down, how bad it'll get. But there are so many other concerns on my mind too, like my business in this shaky economy, and now I'm gonna make my exit? It's the worst timing possible for my son, Cole, to take over. And my little girl, she's twenty-one, but she still just seems like a kid to me. I don't know how she's gonna get through it. She'll have her brother to help her, but he's just a kid himself. Their mother, well, she took the money and ran after our divorce seven years ago, so there's no support for them there. I just needed more time, you know? I just wanted more time." Jim unconsciously picked at the top edge of the thin, white hospital blanket.

Lane leaned in toward him from her seat on the bedside chair. "I can understand that you've got quite a few concerns weighing heavy on your mind right now. Thank you for your honesty. You have much to consider, which will require us to talk about logistics and planning, which I'm sure is well within your comfort zone. It will also be important, however, for us to discuss some more reflective issues related to your relationship with your children, because the insights you uncover during these conversations may very well inform the logistical decisions. Proper progression through this legacy process requires honesty with yourself and with me, so I won't need for you to polish up your thoughts before they leave your mouth. We have indeed run out of time for that."

"I understand," Jim replied, beginning to realize that this process might be very different than what he had imagined.

"If I may ask, Jim, are you a gambler?"

Caught off-guard, he blurted, "What? Um, no, not really."

"You're polishing already."

"Okay, sorry. Yeah, occasionally," Jim said with a sheepish grin, having already been caught in a harmless lie. "I've been known to bring in some serious money at the blackjack table."

"I appreciate your honesty," Lane replied. Her eyes smiled, but her face remained unchanged.

"Well, regardless of your gambling history, Jim, life has dealt you a particular hand of cards, as it has for all of us. The tricky part is that some cards affecting our game, much like the dealer's face-down card in a hand of blackjack, remain hidden. In the game of life, one of these hidden cards is the one that holds the time of our exit from this world—the final card you might say. Most people outright ignore it, playing their hand as if this card didn't exist. Others can't seem to play any cards in their hand effectively, fearing what fate that hidden card may hold. Still others, card counters, play their hand on a best-guess gamble of that hidden death card. Car accident? Terrorist Attack? Cancer."

It was a CT scan machine that had revealed Jim's hidden card years earlier than he'd anticipated.

The consultant continued, "The difficult reality is that the hidden death card does indeed exist for us all, especially for people who hold substantial wealth. Planning for this reality has many advantages, especially for those who want to leave a beneficial legacy. I can see that your financial legacy is very important to you. I have worked with hundreds of clients and rarely do I see an estate so well-planned and frankly, so complicated."

"Yes, that's my attorney, Frank. He's one of the best in the country. He works hand-in-hand with my financial planners, and I'm really proud of how my kids will be set up for the future," Jim replied.

"I wonder, have you put the same level of thought and planning into passing down to your children an inheritance of the other areas of capital?" Lane questioned.

"I'm sorry. I'm not sure what you mean," Jim admitted, confused.

"A person's legacy is multifaceted, although most people get caught up in focusing exclusively on the financial capital portion of their legacy. Droves of people march into the offices of financial planners with lofty goals of extending their wealth for generations. They have cutting-edge estate planning. They pay hundreds of thousands of dollars for top-notch investment management. They send heirs to financial planning education classes. And then they go to sleep at night feeling like they've hedged their bet against that hidden death card. They feel that even if they die young, their heirs will be taken care of financially—their hard-earned wealth will live on as a legacy to their family."

"Yes, that's right. I guess that's me. What's wrong with that? You said my estate plan was impressive!"

"This financial capital is certainly one of the cards you have contributed to your heirs' hand of cards, isn't it? And what a great blessing this card could be to them! Are you aware, however, that research indicates that by the second generation, seventy percent of inherited wealth is completely gone? Within three generations, ninety percent of inherited wealth is lost. There is only a ten percent chance that your great-grandchildren will see any benefit from all of your hard work."[1]

"And I thought my doctors had bad news!" Jim made an attempt to insulate the blow of her words, which hit hard in his gut.

"Rest assured, our work together will substantially increase the odds of your heirs handling their inheritance successfully. In order to provide a framework for our work together, let's get back to our metaphor of playing cards. Your children hold a 'substantial financial capital' card. I would ask you to consider what other cards they hold in their hands. As I recall, an ace has much more value alongside a jack in the game of blackjack, does it not? The work we will do together, integrated legacy planning, considers all the cards and maximizes their potential as they interplay together. Your legacy includes so much more than just financial capital, Jim. It encompasses all aspects of your legacy." Lane continued defining each type of capital to Jim, rattling off a series of questions.[2]

Financial capital: What is your net worth? How much value do you have in cash, investments, real estate, collectibles, art, vehicles, insurance, businesses, or other income? What legal entities or estate-planning instruments have you developed to contain and preserve your financial capital?

Intellectual capital: What value do you place on lifelong learning? How much time do you spend pursuing your own growth and learning, thereby modeling this value? In what ways do you invest time and money in support of the education of others? When was the last intellectual conversation you shared with one of your heirs?

Social capital: How have you been intentional about forging relationships with others? What is the impact of your investment of time with friends and other people in your community? How developed is your social & emotional intelligence (which business research has found to be far more indicative of success than IQ or formal education)?[3] What steps have you taken to teach your heirs' good relational skills? What repair attempts have you made to mend areas of damaged relationship?

Human capital: What energizes you? What skills, passions, talents, idiosyncrasies, or achievements are you known for possessing? How do you share these with your loved ones? How do you foster the development and application of your loved ones' unique skills, talents, idiosyncrasies, achievements, and knowledge?

Spiritual capital: What is the purpose of your life? What cause or belief would you die to defend? What do you believe about the afterlife? What activities or conversations (religious services, prayer, scripture study, meditation, and so on) do you engage in regularly that serve to pass on these spiritual constructs? Can you describe any serendipitous moments in your life where you felt a spiritual guidance that inspired you to make significant personal development? How do you give your time, talents, influence, or money freely for the benefit of others? In what ways have you passed on the value of giving back? How do you strive for balance and peace in your life?

After rattling off the list of questions to illustrate each capital area, Lane pulled out five notecards and wrote one aspect of legacy on each card:

Financial
Intellectual
Social
Human
Spiritual

She gave the stack of cards to Jim and asked him to consider, as he chose how he would spend his remaining time, which aspects of legacy he was intentionally investing in at any given moment. He wasn't sure if she was asking him to literally pull out these cards throughout the day or if she was being figurative, so he asked.

"Jim, if you're pulling out notecards all day long, I fear folks will assume your cancer has made you loopy." Her eyes smiled again, and this time, the corners of her mouth even curled up into the tiniest hint of a smile. "Throughout the day, when you have a moment to yourself, take any one card and write a short note to remind yourself what you did to invest in that area of your legacy. Your notes are just to spark your memory. I'd like you to consider how diversified your energy investments are in each type of capital. For instance, if you had to give an account of the percentage you've invested in each legacy area, you might conclude that you are only 10 percent invested in one and would like to increase your overall investment there. Perhaps you might find you are overinvested in another legacy area and can pull back there."

Overwhelmed but intrigued, Jim was beginning to understand the need for integrated legacy planning, but he figured he had started too late for any of this to be effective. When faced with the reality of his death, he realized that, in attempting to create greater financial capital for his family, he may have missed the very conversations and shared experiences necessary to prepare them to successfully handle it.

"With all due respect, isn't all this too little, too late?"

"Jim, I expect you've not lived a perfect life, and I'm certain you have some regrets, but this makes you no different from scores of other people with terminal cancer. What sets you apart, however, is this process—if you choose to allow it to impact your final days. People hang on every last word of a dying man. You have more influence now than you have ever had. You can't erase your regrets about the past, but you can be intentional about how you spend your remaining time. Hopefully, you will spend it maximizing your intended legacy."

Starting to feel more confident, Jim replied, "I think this may help me leave everyone better prepared for my absence."

"Perhaps, but this process won't be easy. Even the most courageous soul shudders when faced with the task of defining his life's legacy. Let's eat this elephant one bite at a time, or maybe two. Between now and our next meeting, I'd also like you to consider this question: After you die, what three words will your loved ones use to describe the man you were...your legacy?"

Lane described words he might choose: adjectives like generous, adventurous, stubborn, and kind, verbs such as fishing, volunteering, or working, or nouns, perhaps faith, integrity, nature, or business.

She continued, "I will warn you that this exercise can be quite uncomfortable because it brings to light the gaps between who you'd hoped to be and who you are in reality. Do be careful to capture a realistic picture of your impact, rather than an idealized one. You may choose to ask your loved ones this question directly, but people often find greater insight from simply using their interactions with loved ones as an indicator."

The confidence Jim was gaining flew out the window and onto the dark streets below. He felt the heat of frustration rising into a headache. "To be honest with you, Lane, I've always found these kinds of exercises to be time-consuming and fruitless. I'm short on time here. I don't have time to fiddle around with notecards and embark on an exhaustive search for three magic words."

"Have you read Socrates, Jim?"

"The philosopher? I've heard of him, of course."

"Then you probably know that he's famous for saying, 'The unexamined life is not worth living.' Perhaps an unexamined life is not worth living because after it ends, it leaves no ripple effect, no echo, no impact on the world at large. If you've lived your whole life and you can't identify three words that typify the impact you have made on anyone, what's the point of having lived it?"

He wanted to fight her on this, but Jim knew she was right. "I must say, the doctor who did my lumbar puncture yesterday was a bit gentler in her approach." He smiled, pressing his hands into the bed to prop himself up a bit higher.

"Well, let's leave the compassion to her, then, shall we?" Lane said with the first full smile that Jim had seen out of her. She continued, "If your hidden death card had revealed 'car accident,' we wouldn't have this luxury of time, would we? Let's begin to think of this time as a blessing, and set you up to go out with a bang. Now, I'm sensing that perhaps you're ready to switch gears and get working on the business planning side of your legacy. Shall we move on?" Lane handed him a stack of papers.

Relieved, Jim laughed and put on his reading glasses, more than ready to get to work.

YOUR MEETING WITH LANE

Each chapter that follows will conclude with "Your Meeting with Lane," a set of discussion questions to consider independently or with a book/discussion group.

1. If you were working with Lane Brock, how comfortable would you be with the conversation and exercises she offered to Jim?

2. Most people, like Jim, have completed some estate planning for the handling of their finances upon their death. In what ways have you planned for the uncertainty of "the hidden death card?" If you died tomorrow, how well-ordered are your financial affairs?

3. If you died tomorrow, how diversified are your investments of energy in the other areas of capital (intellectual, social, human, spiritual) that you will leave behind? In what area do you need to invest more heavily? How will you accomplish this goal? In what area have you perhaps over invested?

4. How will your investments in these other types of capital prepare your heirs to more effectively handle the financial capital you will leave behind?

5. If your loved ones were asked to describe you in three words, what might they say?

1993

Superman

Vulnerability is not a weakness.
And that myth is profoundly dangerous…
Vulnerability is the glue that holds relationships together.
It's the magic sauce.
—Brené Brown

"How does he look? Does he look, like, normal? Or does he have tubes in his nose and everything?" Campbell, often mature beyond her years, had never felt as naive or unprepared as she did standing outside her father's hospital room.

"He looks fine," Cole assured her. "It's actually hard to believe he only has a few months to live. The ten pounds he's lost recently are the only indication that he's even sick. Get in there, Cammie. He's excited to see you."

Campbell hugged her brother and breathed in the smell of musky gel in his short blonde curls. When she pulled back, she noticed his perfectly clean-cut, polished style was a bit out of sorts. His shirt was untucked, his eyes puffy.

"Hey, are you okay? Did you sleep at all last night?" Campbell tugged the bottom of his oxford shirttail.

"Sleep? Who has time for that? I went home but I couldn't sleep, so I went back to work to tackle this computer glitch we've been having in the warehouse."

"Cole, you've got to take better care of yourself! All this stress, and then no sleep? You should go back to your condo and get some rest," she said, grabbing his coffee and taking a sip from the white plastic lid. "Look, I know these hospital cappuccinos are delicious, but they are NOT a substitute for sleep." She handed the coffee back to him and then poked him in the side. "Hey, there's a double shot of espresso in there. I can taste it! How do you drink that?"

Cole deflected with a sly smile, ignoring her badgering. "So, I'm going back to work for a few hours. You're staying here with Dad all day, right?" He was so grateful his sister had come home. Everything seemed simpler when Campbell was around. She always brought a sense of peace and positivity with her, even now.

"Yes, I'll be here, don't worry! And I'm calling you at 6 p.m. to make sure you are leaving work to go home and eat a good meal, and get some rest!"

As Campbell watched her brother walk down the shiny, white-tiled hallway, she made a mental note to remember to call him later. Who would look out for him if she didn't? He rarely made time to foster friendships or dating relationships, and he took life so seriously. Campbell turned and focused her attention on the hospital room door. She pushed open the door slowly and walked through it with her stomach tied in knots of dread, excitement, and sadness.

40

With no proper script for such moments, Campbell and her father met glances and grasped for words to drown out the harsh reality pressing into their chests.

"Hey, look at that Florida suntan. Have you been at college, or at the beach?" Jim joked.

"Daddy, I've got As in every class, so enough about my sun-kissed skin!" Campbell retorted, kissing his forehead.

"Great job, Cammie. And, hey, I may have a suntan of my own real soon. The doctors should be coming to get me any minute here for my first radiation treatment. I'll go five days a week, and the doctor says that'll buy me a little more time to get things together."

"Daddy..." Campbell teared up at their first joint acknowledgment of the somber elephant in the room.

"Ugh...I know. This whole thing has been such a shock. Hard to wrap your mind around any of it, but we've got to stay focused and think ahead about how to use the time we've got left." Jim pulled himself together quickly, desperate to sweep his daughter safely away from the wave of deep emotion sweeping through the small, sterile room.

There was so much she wanted to say, to ask him:

Are you in pain?
What will the radiation do to your mind?
Are you scared to die?
Will you get to come home from the hospital?
This isn't fair.
I love you.
What will I do without you?
I'm not leaving you to go back to college.

As she struggled to give words to the sentiment filling the heavy space between them, a wheelchair popped into the room, followed by a cheerful man in scrubs, arriving to take her dad to the suntan room.

"Darn. I was afraid this would happen. It looks like I've got to go to radiation. Listen, I'm so glad you're here, Cammie. I'll be back after my treatment is done. Go downstairs and eat some breakfast. I need to tell you, Cynthia hired a consultant. Her name is Lane Brock, and you're scheduled to meet with her at 10 a.m. in the cafeteria. She's going to help me wrap up my affairs. I don't know what information she'll need, but feel free to answer any questions she may have for you."

"Do you need me to go with you to radiation? Can I go with my dad?" Campbell asked, looking over at the man behind the wheelchair.

"Well, darlin', you are more than welcome to walk with us downstairs to the radiation department, but your daddy's going right into the treatment room, and family members aren't allowed in there. He's getting fit for his radiation mask this morning, so it may take a while. I'm really sorry you won't get to see your daddy looking like Superman with that mask on, but you can meet him right back up here in his room in a couple hours. Meantime, I'll take real good care of him." The kindness behind the man's out-of-place southern accent gave Campbell some assurance, although she hated the thought of her father having to endure the treatment alone.

The sight of her father in a wheelchair, wearing a hospital gown, being wheeled down the long hallways made her stomach feel sick. The reality of it. The exposure of it. The helplessness of it. If this experience was hard for her, she imagined how hard it was for him. Cutting the thick emotion in the small elevator, Campbell spoke. "You said my dad was being fitted for his Superman mask. Sorry to be such a stickler, but I'm pretty sure that Superman is one of the only superheroes that doesn't have a mask."

The orderly giggled with embarrassment. "Well, you don't miss a thing, do you? Thank you! Do you know, I have said that to patients at least a dozen times and no one has ever pointed that out. I need to start calling it a Spiderman mask, I suppose!"

Jim chimed in, "Just imagine raising a daughter like this—it's exhausting!" Pride poured from his eyes as he looked up at both of them and gave Campbell a wink.

The elevator doors opened to reveal the radiation department.

"All right, this is our stop. I pushed the button to take you back up to the second floor. That's where you'll find the cafeteria. It was a pleasure to meet you, Campbell."

Popping a kiss on Jim's forehead, Campbell patted the kind orderly on the arm. As she watched her father roll away, the emotion she had been masking for her father's sake re-surfaced. She held back her tears until the elevator doors had closed.

Finding composure and the comfort of brown-sugar-laden oatmeal, Campbell sat in a cold plastic chair in the hospital cafeteria, distracted by a million tiny worries. More than anything, she was gripped by the fear of realizing that she would soon be without the one person she needed in this world. Without her dad, she didn't know how to get through life. She depended on him for everything.

Daddy, my car is making this weird rattle.

43

Hey, Dad, did you have Cynthia buy my airplane tickets for Christmas break?

The doctor's office sent me this bill. What should I do with it?

A sense of shame and embarrassment swept through her as she realized she knew nothing about health insurance. Did the school automatically issue student health insurance? Was it purchased through her dad? If so, how would his death impact all of that? She wondered if her brother, Cole, would be able to help her with the litany of small details that had become the Grand Canyon in her mind. On the other hand, the last thing she wanted to do was bring her brother any more stress.

Desperate to clear her mind, she grabbed her backpack, pulled out her philosophy textbook, and began reading. Minutes ticked by, and she lost track of time.

"Hello, my name is Lane Brock. You are Campbell, I presume? I believe we are scheduled to meet at 10 a.m."

"Oh, gosh. I'm so sorry! I got to reading and must have lost track of the time," Campbell said, glancing down at her watch, which read six minutes past ten. She closed her textbook and slid it into her backpack.

"It's no trouble, really. You're the only female under age fifty in the cafeteria, so I had no trouble finding you. May I ask what you were reading?"

"Søren Kierkegaard. It's for school." Campbell replied, motioning for Lane to sit in the chair across the table.

"Kierkegaard? Well, isn't that serendipitous!" Lane sat down and set her clipboard on the table between them.

"Serendipitous?" Campbell looked up, confused.

Lane spouted off a definition just like an English teacher.

"Serendipity: stumbling fortuitously upon just something that fits perfectly and unexpectedly into your current circumstance."

Campbell smiled. "Hours of SAT prep in high school taught me what 'serendipitous' means. I just don't know why my reading Kierkegaard is serendipitous."

"Well, then I suspect you've just begun your journey with Kierkegaard, or you'd already have discovered that you and he have much in common." Lane's British accent had waned slightly after decades in the US, but her way of putting words together gave her away.

"Oh, right. We are covering all the popular philosophers, and we just got to Kierkegaard."

"You'll learn that it is serendipitous because he, too, was the youngest child in his family, and he lost his father in his twenties, inheriting substantial wealth for the time," Lane revealed.

"Oh really? I didn't know that."

"When serendipity strikes so strong in one's life, it's wise to take notice. I suspect that what you'll learn from your reading of Kierkegaard has the potential to influence the course of your life, if you allow it to settle in." Lane's words danced in the air. Campbell wasn't sure what to make of this woman. She wasn't like any other person her father had hired in the past.

"It does seem like a coincidence that I'm reading Kierkegaard now with everything that is going on with my dad. I didn't realize his dad died young too, so I guess there's probably something there to discover."

"I expect there is as well. And for everything that is going on with your dad, I expect there is also much going on with you." Lane offered the invitation to talk and Campbell accepted, feeling hopeful that this hour with Lane would help her navigate this difficult time.

"It's like a bad dream. I keep thinking I'm gonna wake up, thankful it wasn't real, but, it is real. I just can't believe it. My dad, he's everything. He's like the rock of our family."

"Tell me what that looks like in your everyday life, to have your father as your 'rock.'"

"Well, when the water gets rough, everyone goes reaching for Jim Hannigan, who always knows what to do and how to take care of everything. What will I do without him? I'm embarrassed to admit this, Ms. Brock, but I don't even pay a single bill myself. I know nothing about insurance or investments or his business. I know I'm not stupid, but I worry that everyone only sees a huge 'clueless' stamp on my forehead when I walk into the room. I'm really worried about that."

"I've worked with these clueless inheritors you describe, and you seem to display qualities quite distinctive from them."

Campbell's bright blue eyes looked up expectantly from the cafeteria table to meet Lane's.

"You've displayed self-awareness. You've admitted, at least to yourself and to me, that you know what you do not know—you are aware of important areas of knowledge deficit. In my experience, those who are truly clueless have no awareness of their state of cluelessness, or are unwilling to admit it to themselves or others. There's a wide gap between being clueless and unprepared. You have erroneously identified yourself as clueless when you are simply unprepared."

"I've never thought of myself as an inheritor, really. That's an even more overwhelming thought. There's so much I don't know."

"I see fear in your eyes, Campbell. You're seeking assurance that you have what it takes to handle this situation."

"Yeah."

"As you've been speaking, you've used a metaphor of being in rough water and your father being a rock to hold onto for security."

"I didn't realize I said that, about rough water, but I guess that's exactly what it feels like." Something about this image seemed to unlock Campbell's mind to understand her fears on a deeper level.

"You're fearful and seeking assurance because you know that your rock is slipping underwater, and you feel a lack of confidence navigating rough waters without that rock to hold onto."

Campbell's chest tightened and she felt hot underneath her T-shirt and cardigan sweater.

Lane continued, "In our work together, you can learn how to build several new rocks to secure yourself. As you build these rocks, you will gain confidence in your ability to manage without your father's daily influence on your life. Of course, one of the rocks will be the strength of your father's legacy, which you will undoubtedly have with you even after his passing. This coaching process will require you to work hard and be brutally honest. Are you able to give me everything you've got during our time together, knowing that it may be uncomfortable at times?"

"Absolutely." Campbell suddenly realized this woman somehow deeply understood her, despite their having just met. She felt confident that Lane could help her navigate this journey, which was apparently taking place out on the metaphorical water? Strange that Lane picked up on that. Even stranger that it hit home in such a real way.

"There it is then. You're motivated. That's another charac- teristic distinguishing you from the clueless inheritors. You're motivated to be a good steward of your father's legacy even before you have a dime of it in your pocketbook."

Encouraged and intrigued, Campbell shared no words in reply but stared directly into the calm comfort of Lane's expressionless face.

After some more questions, Lane ended the meeting with a request. "There is an assessment I would like you to complete. It will measure your social and emotional intel- ligence quotient and help us to get a feel for your strengths and development areas.[1] I'd like you to complete it by to- morrow afternoon when we'll have our next meeting."

"That shouldn't be a problem. I'll make time."

"Thank you. I very much enjoyed meeting you. Goodbye, Campbell."

"Goodbye, Ms. Brock."

"Please call me Lane," she called out over her shoulder as she exited.

Really? That was it? That was the meeting?

Campbell was struck by how informal her time with Ms. Brock—Lane—had felt. What had they accomplished? She wasn't sure what she had expected from their first meeting, but Lane Brock and her approach were certainly a surprise. A pleasant surprise, actually.

And what was all this talk of inheritance? Sure, Campbell knew her father was a business owner, but she never thought that had much to do with her. Everyone knew Cole would take over the business. Campbell had about as much inter- est in the automotive industry as Cole had in her beloved passion, writing. She assumed that whatever money her father held would be split between her and her brother, but she had no way of conceptualizing what was about to fall down from the sky into her unsuspecting lap.

Campbell opened her philosophy book and began reading, twirling the end of her yellow highlighter through her shiny hair. Normally, she would be highlighting material she thought might be on the test, but doubting she'd return to school this semester, she read the text like it was written for her. She read and reread one specific line, which seemed to jump off the page, just as Lane had predicted.

"The most common form of despair is not being who you are."[2]

She tried to apply it to her life or current situation, but the quotation was a puzzle piece that didn't seem to fit anywhere, though somehow she knew it was a key piece. Fishing around to find a notecard from her messy backpack, she scribbled down the quotation and tipped back her last sip of coffee. She placed the notecard in the front pocket of her backpack and made her way back upstairs to her father's hospital room.

"The most common form of despair is not being who you are." Campbell's mind reeled. "Not being who you are…Who am I?"

I'm a college student whose dad will be dead in six months.

I'm a writer. Well, not really, but one day, hopefully.

I'm a daughter who wants to take care of her dying dad.

I'm just a kid, in some ways, who won't find the least bit of help or security from her mother through this mess.

I'm not clueless, but unprepared.

I'm losing my rock, but can learn how to build other ways to stabilize myself.

What remained of the day brought a steady stream of physical therapists, neurologists, nurses, and a couple of visits from a doctor who called himself the "quarterback" of Jim's care. Each medical professional echoed the same sentiment:

"Preserve quality of life."

"Make the best of the time that remains."

"Do our best to keep you comfortable."

It was so overwhelming. Jim and Campbell both fought back strong emotions in an effort to be strong for the other. Each time one doctor would leave they would look at each other with eyes wide, sad and scared.

Campbell breathed in courage from the dry hospital air and broached a tense subject. "Dad, do you have a plan for who will care for you…like…in the end?"

"Oh, that's what hospice is for, Cammie, and your brother will be around to make sure we've got the best people on our team." Jim addressed the issue as if they were discussing the creation of a new department at Hannigan Industries.

"Daddy, you'll need family around—people you're comfortable with. It sounds like it could get really hard. I want to be the one to help you through this. I'm—I'm not going back to school. I want to be with you, and I want to be the one to take care of you." Campbell laid down her final decision, gentle yet firm.

"No ma'am. I am not allowing this situation to knock you off your course. You'll go back to school, and you'll finish the semester." Jim pointed his finger like he used to do when he disciplined her childhood misbehavior.

The tears she'd been holding back started streaming down her face. She gripped the rail at the foot of the hospital bed with both hands, looking squarely at her father who refused to return her gaze. "Daddy, this isn't a situation. You are dying! Do you understand that? In less than six months! If I go back to school, I may never see you again. College will still be here in six months! You won't. I'm staying with you."

Staring out the window, Jim replied sharply but with a detached, flat tone. "I'm afraid that it will get very bad in the end, Campbell, and I don't want you to see that. It's hard to shake that kind of thing from your mind. I'm trying to protect you from it. Go. Back. To school!"

"Don't you get it? You can't protect me from this! You're not doing this alone. I'm going to be with you, and you can't stop me."

Cupping his hand over his closed eyes, Jim sat thoughtfully for a moment and then said quietly, "You are so stubborn."

Campbell walked around to the side of the bed and sat down, forcing eye contact. "I learned it from you." She put her lips on his forehead and kept them there. Jim's chest began to tremble, and for the first time ever, Campbell was witness to her father's tears.

As they cried together in silence, it seemed like time had stopped.

Finally, wiping his eyes, Jim pulled himself together. "Okay, okay, enough of that sappy stuff. I'm exhausted, and I'm sure you are too. Why don't you go home, get some rest, and come back in the morning."

Campbell pulled back, and as she looked deeply into her father's tearstained face, a surprising insight entered her mind. The orderly was right about her father wearing a Superman mask after all. Maybe Clark Kent didn't wear a mask, but Jim Hannigan did. He had always tried so hard to protect her and her brother from the brunt of the challenges they'd faced, especially through their parents' divorce and estrangement from their mother. The truth was that she only knew half of this man. He had always hidden his struggles, his weakness, his vulnerabilities, his failures. He wore his mask out of love for them. Now, for the first time, she could see behind his mask.

"I will leave, if you promise me that when I come back tomorrow you won't be wearing your Superman mask."

Confused, Jim replied, "Superman doesn't wear a mask. Remember, smarty pants? And they keep my mask in the radiation room, so you'll never see it."

Campbell giggled and brushed her hair from her face, tucking it behind her ear. "No, Dad, what I mean is, right now you're being real with me. I can see behind the Superman mask you always wear with Cole and me; you know, tough Dad who's always in control? Well, you're not in control now. You're scared and frustrated, and that seems perfectly normal to me. I just want you to know that it's okay to be real with me. Listen, I know you'll always see me as your little girl, but I am officially an adult now. When you are in pain, I need to know that. When you're scared, say so and we'll talk about it. If you're tired and want to me to go away, please tell me. I can handle whatever you throw at me, Dad. When you try to protect me from hard paths in life, both of us miss out on the journey of finding our way through it together."

Still feeling emotional, Jim sat speechless and just nodded his head to his daughter. She squeezed his hand, said goodnight, and left him alone to process all that she had shared.

Campbell walked through the hospital halls, fumbling to find the keys to her father's car inside her backpack. Arriving home, she glanced at the clock, which read 6 p.m., and called Cole at home first and then at work. Troubled to hear that he was still at work, Campbell knew he was pushing himself too hard. He promised her he would leave for home in a half hour. "Where is he getting all this energy?" she wondered.

Campbell was exhausted, but figuring she'd never be able to sleep, she met up with some old high school friends at the corner bar.

"I can't believe your dad is dying, Campbell."

"How are you handling this?"

"We are way too young to have our parents die!"

Campbell had hoped to find comfort in their presence, but there was something cold in her friends' expressions of sympathy. Ironically, she found herself offering comfort to them with quips about staying positive, looking at the bright side, and finding inner strength in tough times.

"Campbell, don't look now, but you won't believe who just walked in," her petite friend exclaimed with a squeal, channeling the middle-school girl still lurking inside her now twenty-something body.

A casual glance over her shoulder revealed Britt Newberry, the handsome and now perfectly matured young man who had been her crush during high school. Being two years older than Campbell, he had one foot on the path to college by the time she caught his attention during the summer after he graduated.

"Campbell Hannigan. Welcome home! Hey, I heard about your dad. I'm so sorry," he said with genuine compassion in his voice. Standing alongside her bar stool, he gently brought her head to his chest with his hand for a moment of comfort. "I'm glad you're out tonight. How's college in the Sunshine State treating you?"

She hadn't gotten this much attention from Britt Newberry in quite some time. The spark between them hadn't had time to build into a respectable fire before he had gone to college. Although she had seen him a handful of times since then, that spark had never reignited until now. She reflected on the uncomfortable fame that came from having a terminally-ill father, realizing that if Britt Newberry already knew, everyone knew.

Less distracted by her grief with each drink, Campbell reveled in the attention Britt poured on her.

"How'd you hear about my dad being sick?"

"My mom told me. Apparently our moms talk sometimes, I guess. They met up last year when my mom visited Chicago, and they've kept up with each other since then."

"Oh, I didn't know that. I don't really talk to my mom that much. So, hey, where are you working now, college graduate?" she asked him, changing the subject.

"Well, I've teamed up with some college buddies to get this internet business off the ground, but in the meantime, I've just been working retail around here. How about you? What's your major?"

"English lit. I want to be a writer or a college professor. Both, really. Although that's the last thing on my mind right now. I can't go back to school this semester. I can't leave my dad."

"Have you asked your dad about that?"

"Yeah, just tonight. I mean…I didn't really ask him. I sort of just told him." A shy smile spread across her lips.

"No one TELLS your dad anything, Campbell. He's the owner of the biggest automotive supply company in Detroit! I'd like to have heard how that conversation went down."

"How can I leave him now, Britt? He doesn't have much time left! I'm not wasting that time back at school when I could be with him. And someone's got to take care of him. It's going to get really bad, you know?"

"I get it, I get it. I'm just sorry you're dealing with all of this." Britt looked around the crowded bar. "Listen, do you want to get outta here, go for a walk or something?" He put his arm around her waist.

Campbell paid her tab, hugged her friends, and made her exit with Britt. As she walked away, the girls couldn't hold back their judgment. Everyone on the outside knew more than Campbell about how well the Hannigan business had done in the past decade. It seemed that their dinner table was the only place there hadn't been a conversation about the fortune she and Cole would likely inherit upon their father's death.

"Well, it looks like Britt Newberry is not as dumb as he looks," one friend said snidely to the other, raising her hand to alert the bartender to her empty glass. "He's all over Campbell, and her dad's not even dead yet. She's the most eligible heiress in town, and she's completely clueless."

Eyeballing Campbell's receipt, the other friend nodded in agreement, adding "I hope she is clueless and not just a tightwad, because I'm pretty sure that a girl who's about to be a millionaire shouldn't leave such a crappy tip. Look at this!"

YOUR MEETING WITH LANE

1. Describe a moment when you experienced serendipity in your life. What did this moment of serendipity teach you?

2. The quote that stood out to Campbell from Kierkegaard's writing was, "The most common form of despair is not being who you are." In what ways can family wealth increase the risk of not being, or knowing, who you are?

3. Jim struggled with the idea that Campbell wanted to be his caregiver instead of going back to college. What plans has your family made, or conversations have you had, about how the end-of-life physical needs of loved ones will be handled?

4. Campbell accuses Jim of wearing a Superman mask, or protecting his children from his own vulnerabilities and other challenging aspects of life. If you have your own children, especially older children, how can you be vulnerable and honest with them about challenging life situations without inappropriately leaning too much on them? In what ways, if any, did your own parents shelter you from the difficult parts of life even into your adulthood? How did this impact you?

5. Campbell's friends were judgmental at the end of the chapter. In what ways can wealth get in the way of relationships? How can people with wealth determine which friends are loyal and genuine, and which are resentful or opportunistic?

2014

Today, I Just Really Miss My Dad

Dad, wherever you are, you are gone,
but you will never be forgotten.
—Conrad Halls

The sun beat down hard on Campbell's head. She reached up to touch the top of her long, thick, strawberry hair, now speckled with gray.

"My hair might actually catch fire. Who in their right mind holds a graduation ceremony outdoors in June in Florida? Come on, kids, let's go find our seats under the tent. I've got to get out of this blazing sun!"

The tented area revealed a stage decorated beautifully with balloons and flowers in the red and white school colors. A gorgeous sign spanning the width of the stage provided a beautiful backdrop across the platform where Campbell's nephew, Tyler, along with the ninety-four other graduates of the private school, would walk to receive his high school diploma.

"Congratulations, Class of 2014."

"What is Mom's deal? She's completely freaking out! Look at her fanning herself at turbo speed."

Campbell looked over at her ninth grade twins with a feigned angry face. "I heard that, young lady. I am NOT freaking out, thank you very much. I'm just hot. Does this look like freaking out to you, Jimmy? Be careful, your sister is apparently a mental health professional now. She'll be diagnosing you any minute too. Are you guys not absolutely melting in this heat?"

Jade and Jimmy snickered at their mother's guilty sarcasm. Campbell put an arm around Jimmy's shoulder and popped each of her children playfully in the head with her event program. She stood up, peering over their heads at the crowd of people moving into the tented area.

"Okay, I admit maybe I am a little amped up this morning. Can you imagine how hard this must be for Tyler, to attend his high-school graduation without his father here? I'm worried about him, and I want the day to be really special for him. I'd like to kick your Uncle Cole in the shins for missing this moment. And where is your father? He's going to be late!"

"Mom, Tyler seemed totally fine this morning. He's good. Don't worry." Jimmy grabbed his mother's hand and guided her back down into her folding chair. "And I texted Dad and told him where we're sitting. He said he was almost here. He's probably in the parking lot now."

"Okay, good. Thanks, honey." Campbell smiled at her beautiful children and took a deep breath, remembering all that she had to be grateful for in her life. Despite the heat of the day, she did love living in Florida, the state where her husband had grown up and built his thriving construction business. Her career was flourishing with an adjunct professor position at the local university and five published books. She had two beautiful children and a loyal, loving husband. She had been given the opportunity to play a vital role in Tyler's life, and she was doing her best to ensure that her nephew would leave her home with the same values she was teaching her own children.

And she had one more year to do it. Because of all that had happened with his father, Tyler agreed that he could benefit from living at home for one more year with Campbell and her family. The University of Central Florida was a good school, only fifteen minutes away, and Tyler could commute until he felt more confident. It was a good plan. There had been moments over the past year and a half that made her doubt this day ever would come, but Tyler was graduating, and he was going to be okay. The resolve she had lost for a brief, hot moment began to resurface, and her thoughts drifted to her father and how proud he would be to share in this moment.

"Hey, pretty lady! I made it, with one minute to spare." Russ dropped into the seat next to her, glancing at his watch, just as the band erupted, signaling the start of the ceremony. He smelled like a fresh shower and his hair was still wet, dark brown curls slicked back and to the side.

Russ whispered in her ear. "Jimmy texted me that you're freaking out. Are you okay?"

"Oh, for heaven's sake, I was just hot!" Campbell whispered, looking up into her husband's doubtful, smiling face. "Okay, the truth is, I was freaking out a little, but I pulled it back together, and I'm good now."

Russ winked and played up the slightly southern accent he'd acquired from his north Florida upbringing. "I think it's pretty sexy when you freak out, babe! It happens so rarely these days. I can't believe I missed it! So, Tyler's doing okay?"

"He seemed fine this morning."

"He's handling things better lately, isn't he?"

Campbell continued fanning herself. "Yeah, I think so."

"And you're good?" Russ checked in again, this time more seriously.

"Yeah, I'm okay. This morning I was upset, just thinking about how sad it is that Cole isn't here for Tyler. But sitting here now, I'm feeling different. Now I'm really wishing that my dad was here. I'd give anything to see Jim Hannigan sitting at his oldest grandson's graduation, just beaming with pride. Most days, I'm okay, but today, I just really miss my dad."

YOUR MEETING WITH LANE

In this flash-forward chapter, we learn that Campbell takes Cole's son, Tyler, into her home and raises him as her own child because Cole is either unable or unwilling to do so. Campbell's willingness to raise her nephew indicates a strong sense of family and a willingness to make sacrifices for family members, despite her feelings about Cole's absence.

1. In what ways does your family teach or model the importance of having a strong family bond and encourage family members to be there for each other during hard times?

2. What gets in the way of your family's desire to support one another, especially those who are struggling?

3. If these values haven't been a top priority in the past, what's one thing you can do in the next month to increase your family's drive to be there for one another?

1993

Making Peace

You must learn to let go. Release the stress.
You were never in control anyway.
—*Steve Maraboli*

"Good morning, Miss Morning. How are you this morning, Miss Morning?" Campbell savored her father's familiar morning greeting, trying to memorize it with all of her senses.

"Good morning, Daddy. I'm a little tired from staying out late with some high school friends, but I'm okay. How are you feeling today?" Campbell shot him her winning smile.

"Seems that when you're dying, all anyone wants to talk about is how you're feeling." Jim winked, protecting his daughter from the knowledge of the rough bout of severe headaches he had endured overnight at the hospital. "Surely there are more important things we can discuss."

"I thought we settled this Superman issue last night!" Campbell put her hands on her hips.

"Oh come on. Let's talk about school. Are you learning anything useful? That business school building is just sitting there waiting for you to take a class there and learn something useful." Jim always pressed the issue of Campbell learning some business sense, but now it felt even more urgent.

"Daddy, are we going to do this again?" She rolled her eyes. From the time she was a little girl, Campbell had dreamed of being a writer and had tired of her father incessantly reminding her that he didn't approve. Jim feared she would lose her direction and flounder like many aspiring writers, especially after she found out how much money she would inherit when he died.

"Campbell, sit down." He touched the side of his bed, urging her to come closer. "Maybe it's been a mistake that I haven't been honest with you about…my financial situation. I've done pretty well in my industry, and I think you're going to be surprised when you see the bottom line. I'm afraid you're unprepared to handle what's falling into your lap here."

With hesitation, Jim whispered as he continued, "Fifty million dollars, Cammie. That's what you've got coming to you. You'll have more in cash and investments than Cole because he's getting the business. Fifty million dollars! Of course, that's before the estate tax, which will cut into a good portion of that amount, but with the changes we're making to my estate plan…"

Overwhelmed, Campbell's concentration drifted away from her father's words.

"Fifty million dollars?" a blurted whisper left her lips as she stood, flabbergasted, and walked over to the window. Anyone else would be ecstatic to hear the number her father was revealing, but the pounding in her heart played a drumbeat, not of excitement, but of fear.

"I never wanted you to think you were any better than anyone else, so we lived like everyone else, but you need to be ready to handle all of this. There will be investment meetings, and accountants, and attorneys, and big decisions to be made. If you had taken some classes, you'd understand all of it."

Putting up her own mask of courage, she snapped back, "Daddy, I'm not stupid, and I'm not a kid anymore. I'll figure it out. Besides, I'm pretty sure I haven't seen 'inheriting substantial wealth' in the business school course catalog."

"No, but at least you'd understand the basics! I worry that the money will make you vulnerable. Boys will want to be with you just for the money. Investment managers could take advantage of your lack of knowledge. I've told your brother to make sure he looks out for you, that I'll haunt him mercilessly if he treats you unfairly, but I just wish you were more knowledgeable in this area."

"You're totally stressing about this, and that's the worst thing for you right now. I'll be fine. I'll figure it out like I always do."

He had to admit, Campbell did have a way of always stumbling her way into success, but this situation was bigger; the stakes were so much higher.

"And don't you think it would be an easier life to just work in the business with Cole? He could use the help, and it would be more reliable work for you. This writing thing can be a hobby for you. I just don't know why you'd bite the hand that feeds you, Cammie! The automotive industry has been good to us. Can't you see that?"

"Daddy, I've wanted to be a writer since I was a little girl. You know that. I appreciate that Detroit has been good to us, but that kind of work will bore me to tears. It might have been your dream, but it's not mine."

"It wasn't a dream. It was a job! It was a way to make a life for you and your brother that was better than the life I had. Life isn't all about what's fun and exciting. It's about working hard and making something of yourself."

"That's your legacy, Dad. I want my legacy to be that I made a difference in peoples' lives by helping them see the beauty and potential in themselves and in the world around them. I'm good at writing and teaching, and that's what I'm going to do."

As the word legacy left Campbell's mouth, Jim remembered the question Lane had asked him to consider.

"After you die, what three words will your loved ones use to describe the man you were - your legacy?"

Jim knew that Campbell saw him as hardworking, but he worried this aspect of his legacy was a value she hadn't internalized, and that really concerned him.

"And as far as dealing with the money and all the business stuff that comes with it, I'll figure it out. Stop worrying. It's not good for you to be worrying so much," Campbell said definitively.

As if on cue, a nurse popped into the room to take Jim's vitals, offering a reprieve from the tense conversation. Jim's blood pressure was elevated, and Campbell guessed hers probably was too. The kind, young nurse encouraged him to relax.

"See, Daddy? I told you it's not good for your body to worry."

Jim took a deep breath in an effort to calm himself, but there was just too much on his mind. Just then, a man appeared over Campbell's shoulder, sticking out his hand toward her.

"Dr. Stern, neurologist. You must be Jim's daughter."

"Campbell Hannigan," she replied, shaking the doctor's enormous hand.

"So, how are you handling the radiation treatments?" the doctor inquired, nodding towards Jim.

Jim looked at Campbell and realized all at once that she was right; there was no way he could protect her from the reality of his illness.

"Actually, it was a pretty rough night, doc. Brutal headaches. Couldn't sleep much because of it. The nurses kept increasing the pain meds, but they didn't seem to touch it."

Looking at his chart, the doctor replied, "I see that. Wow, I'm surprised that dose of medicine didn't take the edge off of the pain. How are you feeling now?"

"The headache is still there, but it's manageable now."

"Well, let's switch the pain med and see if that helps. Unfortunately, the headaches, fatigue, hair loss, and perhaps a bit of short-term memory loss are all part of the experience, but we will help you to manage it the best we can." The doctor exited with the same swiftness as he entered.

"I'm sorry you're having bad headaches, Daddy. You didn't say anything." Campbell went to the sink to prepare a cold washcloth. She folded it and gently placed it on his forehead. Savoring his daughter's care and the brief respite from his gripping headache, Jim closed his eyes and admitted to himself that Campbell understood people, understood life, understood love in a way that he couldn't. Maybe she wasn't cut out to work in the business. Maybe she could find success on the path of her dreams. He certainly wasn't able to stop her from putting her life on hold for him now, nor from being exactly the woman she wanted to be. He figured he might as well learn to work with the person she was instead of trying to change her. And right now, she seemed to be exactly what he needed.

"Thank you, Cammie. That feels much better. Where'd you learn to be so caring? Must have been from your mother's side of the family, because it sure wasn't from me."

"I think we both know we can't give credit to Mom for that! You're a caring man, Daddy. You just have an unconventional way of showing it. I mean, really, do you think I could have attended the dozens of charity functions you made me attend as your date and not left with a little heart?"

He lifted the washcloth and peeked up at her. "Hey, speaking of your mother, have you heard from her? I'm sure she will be circling like a vulture to see if there's any more money to scavenge."

"Yeah, she called me yesterday. I had to talk her out of boarding the next train from Chicago to Detroit."

"You know you won't be able to keep her away."

"She does sound legitimately concerned about you, and she's sad just like the rest of us."

"Campbell, this is exactly what I'm talking about! You need to realize that you are becoming very vulnerable to being taken advantage of by people. Even your mother. Especially your mother!"

"Dad, your blood pressure! Relax, and stop worrying!" Campbell flipped on the small TV in his hospital room, finding a news program to distract him.

One thing she didn't need right now was her divorced parents' drama creating extra stress. She never wanted to know all the details, but Campbell did know that her father had cheated on her mother multiple times. Her mother made certain that everyone knew about that. She also knew that her mother was no angel. Campbell and Cole had seen her true colors when their mother had negotiated more money in the divorce settlement in exchange for conceding full custody to Jim, justifying that she had 'earned it' after all Jim had put her through during their marriage.

Her mother had left the day before Campbell's twelfth birthday to move to an apartment outside Chicago with her high-school boyfriend, a used car salesman. The two of them were living off her five million dollar divorce settlement in a pathetic, flashy, and trashy sort of way.

Cole hadn't spoken to their mother since the day she left and he referred to her not as "Mom," but "Debbie." All of Debbie's cards, gifts, and telephone calls to Cole had been ignored. For Cole, there had been a clean break in his relationship with his mother. For Campbell, it was more complicated. She didn't respect her mother, but she couldn't stand the thought of not speaking to her. Their relationship was mostly superficial, but at least they still had some connection. Any resentment she had toward her mother for leaving and for choosing the money over her own children, Campbell buried to keep the peace. Although she and Cole had felt like commodities, bought and sold in the divorce decree, she had settled on feeling content to have at least one parent willing to maintain a stable home for them. She looked over at her dad watching the television, pleased that her plan to distract him had been successful.

"I'm going to go grab a coffee from downstairs before my meeting with Lane. Everything's gonna be good, okay? No more worrying!"

"Cammie, please address her as Ms. Brock. She's a professional. Don't call her Lane."

"She told me to call her Lane!" Campbell said, popping her head back around the room's privacy curtain.

"Really? I'm not sure I even feel comfortable calling her Lane. She's pretty intimidating, isn't she?"

"I actually really liked her!"

"Really? Well, have a good meeting, I guess."

As Jim watched Campbell walk out the door, he thought about Lane Brock and all she had stirred inside him. What was it about her that he found so intimidating? Was it her British accent? Her stern yet kind approach? If he was honest, it was possibly her beauty that intimidated him. Jim had no trouble with women, and they were usually the ones intimidated by him. He relished the game of watching them move from being nervous and acquiescent about dating the owner of Hannigan Industries, to, after a few dates, becoming proud, confident, and unrestrained. This stage was his favorite part, for obvious reasons, but it was always over too quickly. Soon, the third and last stage would begin. They would start putting expectations on his time, complaining that he was emotionally unavailable and always distracted by work. In honest moments, he could admit that there was a long list of women he'd hurt by his inconsistent need for female affection. Somehow, now, he felt rising regret for these actions that had seemed playful and harmless before. No matter what the motivation, he wanted to at least make an attempt to complete the tasks Lane had assigned to him.

He pulled out the notecards she had given him and read each one, considering what elements of his conversation with his daughter he might write on each one.

Financial: warned her about vulnerabilities with the inheritance she'll be receiving; told her it would be better to work for the family business

Intellectual: reinforced importance of education in financial matters

Social: told her to be wary of her mother

Human: she cared for my headache

Spiritual: she said my charity events taught her to have heart

Jim wasn't sure he even totally understood how to fill out these cards. Figuring he had done all right, he put his cards away for now. He also needed to identify those three words about his legacy. Campbell had called him hardworking, and that was certainly a trait he hoped to pass down. Cole seemed to have acquired it, motivated and working late hours under his father to learn the business.

Hardworking.

Campbell had also called him stubborn. Perhaps that was true too. In fact, he admitted to himself, he derived some pride from being called stubborn. He wrote both words on the list he owed to Ms. Brock—Lane.

Hardworking. Stubborn.

And heart. Unexpectedly, she had given him the credit for her compassionate heart. It felt good to know that she saw him in this light.

Heart.

He swung his legs out of bed. Now what? A self-professed type-A control freak, Jim didn't know what to do with himself stuck in the tiny hospital room. He had tired of the news programs, which seemed to inflate and regurgitate the same stories again and again. Agitated, the movement of his eyes matched the harried speed of his brain. Finally, his gaze stopped upon the one framed painting that adorned the sterile, white walls.

A sailboat.

"Well, how about that?" he whispered to himself.

Jim rarely took time for himself, for hobbies, but when he did, he could be found out on the water, sailing. It was the only place he could truly relax and unwind. The expanse of clear blue water separated him from the worries and the work that gripped him on land. The wind through his strawberry blond, now graying, hair carried away the concerns weighing heavy on his mind, and helped him think clearly. Sometimes he worked on the boat, taking customers out in an effort to close the deal, but it was when he was out on the water all alone that he could really find himself.

The cheaply-framed print of Claude Monet's *The Bridge at Argenteuil* stared back at him as if it had something to say.

He pulled himself up out of the bed to take a closer look. For a few brief moments, there was no worry, no cancer, no regret, just Jim lost in his thoughts on a sailboat, nautical miles from the hospital.

Jim had never been a religious man. Although he checked the Christian box whenever it appeared, he had found church to be mostly a waste of time and a distraction from the truth in his heart. If Jim was honest, the notion of handing over any bit of control to an unseen divine was simply too far out of his nature. Of course, there was something humbling about a terminal diagnosis; it flashed a neon sign screaming the harsh reality that he was clearly not in control. The only time Jim ever felt connected to God was out on the open water. Now, he was deeply drawn to this print, and even more deeply drawn to the idea that God was somehow still in control over his life, his children's lives, and the future.

Soul trembling, he quietly whispered the prayer he'd recited so many nights over the water before he went to sleep on the sailboat:

"Dear God,
Be good to me.
The sea is so wide
And my boat is so small.[1] *"*

YOUR MEETING WITH LANE

Jim's hopes for Campbell's future differed drastically from her plans, which is not uncommon with parents and their young-adult children.

1. What advice would you give to Jim?

2. What advice would you give to Campbell?

3. What piece of this advice can you apply to your own life?

4. Jim had a serendipitous moment when he noticed the art print in his hospital room. What insights do you think he had in that moment?

5. In this moment, Jim realized he had neglected to make significant investments of spiritual capital with Cole and Campbell. In what ways does your family invest in spiritual capital?

6. Reflect back on Jim's favorite prayer. What was it about this prayer that was so meaningful to him? How did the meaning of this prayer change for him, in light of his terminal diagnosis?

1993

Resistance

We have been to the moon,
we have charted the depths of the ocean and the heart of the atom,
but we have a fear of looking inward to ourselves
because we sense that is where all the contradictions flow together.
—*Terence McKenna*

There had been little time for Cole to sleep since his father's diagnosis, but even in quiet moments, sleep wouldn't come. Staring into the darkness, he drowned a million worries in the sprawling, 500-gallon built-in saltwater fish tank, an impressive centerpiece in his new, posh, downtown penthouse.

What was the best plan for communicating the news of his father's diagnosis to the company, to the customers? He'd have to consult with his father. Ultimately, it was Jim's decision, but Cole imagined himself delivering the news, a first show of strength as the owner of the company.

Would the employees give him the respect needed to run the business? He'd have to earn it, and that wouldn't be easy since several of the long-time employees had been working there since Cole was a just a toddler.

Could he allay customers' fears that the company would flounder under his leadership? He'd have to become more social and he'd have to do some schmoozing, neither of which came naturally to him. Cole always had confidence in his intellect, but it had taken until college for him to gain any social confidence. A late bloomer, he had finally filled out in college, surprising even himself when a new, handsome, and almost rugged physique replaced the skinny, nerdy appearance he had in high school. The new look helped with the girls and made him more comfortable socially, but there was part of him that still felt anxious in social settings, though he would never admit it. After all, it was nothing that a well-timed shot of whiskey couldn't fix.

What could he do to keep the business thriving through the transition? Diversify. Maybe he should diversify. The automotive companies were looking to new technologies, and he'd be damned if he was going to leave the future of his business in their hands. He would make whatever innovations necessary to ensure that Hannigan Industries would continue to be the number-one automotive supplier in Detroit.

How would he go about phasing out his father's advisors? They had always been too conservative, and Cole would have to bring in people that matched his style of doing business. Jim had been successful, but Cole secretly questioned many of his father's conservative business and investment approaches. His dad had experience, but Cole had education and the stomach for a bit more risk. Times were changing in the industry, and maybe Cole's innovation was just what the company needed. There was plenty of time to make these changes, but he should start researching some new hires.

The alarm clock rang out from the bedroom, interrupting his thoughts. 4:30 a.m. He silenced the harsh beeping and went to the kitchen to make some coffee. He usually loved mornings. He had never been able to sleep in late, anticipating all that could be accomplished in the day ahead. Campbell, on the other hand, had preferred to sleep the whole morning away, Cole recalled, thinking back to the days when they lived at home together.

Lately, mornings had been rough for Cole. Even on the rare nights when he was able to get some sleep, he woke to the harsh reality that everything had changed.

His dad was dying. Dying young. Would this mean he, himself, was likely to have cancer at a young age? Was he likely to die young? Was Campbell?

He wasn't sure how Campbell would handle these concerns, but he knew he'd be fine. He had powered through other challenges in the past. His mother's meltdown. His parents' divorce. And now this.

Every time he'd faced a challenge in the past, he'd put his nose to the grindstone and pushed past it. This time, he would do the same. Work hard. Push past it.

Cole squeezed a pill bottle between his hands, spinning open the white cap. The shoulder injury he'd incurred in college intramural sports still gave him trouble, especially when he wasn't sleeping well. It had been several months since he'd needed the painkillers, but since his father's diagnosis, he had begun taking at least two pills across the day. He swirled the bottle, enjoying the sound of the pills against the plastic, eyeballing the number that remained. He pulled one out between his thumb and forefinger and swallowed it with his coffee, breathing in deep, readying himself to start the day.

Three hours sitting in front of his office computer flew by in minutes but left him with a very stiff neck. Remembering his meeting with Lane Brock, he tried to clear a space on his desk for her, and then decided they would meet in the conference room. Cole was known for his extremely messy office, but he prided himself on always knowing just where everything was. In his mind, he simply had a different method of organization, and as long as it was working for him, there was no need to change.

Cole phoned his father's assistant, Cynthia, requesting that she bring Lane Brock and two cups of coffee to the conference room for their meeting.

"Good morning, Ms. Brock. Sorry, I'm a few minutes late. I see Cynthia got you some coffee."

"Please call me Lane. Cynthia was kind enough to bring me some tea, actually."

"Oh, right. Brits drink tea. What was I thinking?"

As Cole got settled into the chair at the head of the conference room table, Lane began, "How are you managing your transition here at work, Cole?"

"Everything's going great!"

"I expect there are certainly challenges, given the circumstances under which you're taking over the business?"

"Well, sure, but overall, I think we've been managing as well as can be expected."

Lane leaned in and pressed further. "And how are you handling your father's illness?"

Cole leaned back, rocking in the black office chair and looking off into the distance. "Having Campbell here is huge. It takes a lot of stress off my plate, having her caregiving for him. I feel a lot better about the whole situation now."

"I see. And how—"

The phone buzzed and Cynthia's voice echoed through the speaker. "Cole, I'm sorry to interrupt. I have Bill from Chrysler on line two. Shall I take a message?"

Cole quickly agreed to answer the call. "Excuse me, Lane. This will just take a minute."

Several minutes passed before the call concluded, and after Cole put down the phone, Lane jumped right back in. "Let's move ahead to our action items for today, then. I've brought with me the results of the emotional intelligence assessment you completed after our first meeting. Here is your copy. You'll see that your scores are listed on a line graph, with strengths listed in green and development areas listed in red. On page three, please note your top three strengths, which I have highlighted. They include achievement drive, initiative, and catalyzing change. You can see that the definitions for each factor are listed there. I wonder, Cole, how do you think these strengths will benefit you during this transition at Hannigan Industries?"

Cole rubbed his chin, perusing his results. "This is good. This seems really good because these are the leadership skills I'll need to run the business. I need to work hard, get things done, be the catalyst for change in the areas that need improvement. I feel really good about this."

"These key strengths of leadership will undoubtedly serve you well in your transition to the owner of this business, and I have seen your father beam with pride and confidence in recognizing these strengths in you. Where did you acquire these strengths?"

"From my dad. I mean, that's how he lived—always working hard. He was always saying these annoying little phases.

He'd wake me up and say, 'The early bird gets the worm! Don't you want to be that early bird?' Campbell drove him crazy because she wanted to sleep in on Saturdays. He'd yell up to her, 'While the rest of the world is out working, you're in there sleeping!' And the cheesiest one was, 'The path to success isn't paved. You've got to clear it yourself with hard work and stick-to-itiveness.'"

"We don't have that word in England, but I like it. That certainly does sound like your father, doesn't it? So you've learned from your father to utilize your strengths of achievement, initiative, and catalyzing change in your work environment. Now tell me, Cole, how do these strengths manifest in your life outside of work?"

"Hm. I haven't had much time for anything outside of work lately."

"Been burning the candle at both ends, have you? Tell me about your social life. Anyone special in your life?"

Cole shook his leg nervously, his heel tapping on the clear plastic mat underneath his chair. "No, I wouldn't make a good husband, and I'm not planning on getting married anyway. After watching my parents' mess of a marriage, I don't want any part of it. Sometimes I'll go out with some buddies to bars and meet girls. I do okay with girls, but even when I go out, it's like a competition to me to see if I can land the hottest girl in the club. I guess you could say I'm a bit of an achievement junkie, even in my social life."

"Our strengths overused become our weaknesses, Cole. Let's flip the page and discuss your weaknesses, or as I prefer to call them, 'development areas.'"

"You'll note that self-control, self-awareness, and interpersonal effectiveness are your lowest areas. This means you may have trouble recognizing your emotions and their impact on your behavior in the moment. You may also have trouble recognizing other people's emotions and responding appropriately to them."

"Yeah. Yeah, that's probably true. I've been told I can be a bit of a steamroller. I'm just trying to move forward, to get things done, and get them done right."

"You called yourself a steamroller. A steamroller moving through your work and personal life could do some serious damage. Look again at the development areas. On a scale of one to ten, how committed are you to working to develop these areas in an effort to minimize their negative impact on your work and personal life?"

"If I'm being honest, it's a low number right now. I have my hands full just keeping the business afloat. Even finding time for this meeting was a challenge! I thought the point of our meetings would be to make plans for the succession of the business, but I can't say I'm committed right now to this big self-improvement gig. Since word got out about my dad's illness, I've had five calls from nonprofits asking if I'll be on their board of directors, eight calls from local sales execs who want to ensure their business will stay with us after I take over, and three calls from opportunistic women who want to know what I'm doing on Saturday night. I'm inundated right now and just don't have the time."

"With all due respect, Cole, this work is the preparation for the business succession plan. The impact of your weaknesses will certainly grow if left unaddressed, especially through this stressful time, and will affect your employees' ability to embrace you as their leader and your ability to lead them effectively."

"Listen, don't get me wrong. I respect your work, Lane. I just see it as something to work on in the future, maybe even the near future. But for now, it's just bad timing."

Lane took a brief moment to place one file in her briefcase and take out another. "I respect your no. Let's discontinue further discussion of this assessment then, with the understanding that we can pick it back up at any time. Would you like to move on to developing the content of your speech at the Hannigan employee meeting next week?"

"I'd like that."

YOUR MEETING WITH LANE

1. What factors may have caused Cole to be so resistant to the developmental process Lane suggested?

2. What problems do you anticipate may occur in Cole's work and personal life if he continues to avoid working on the concerns Lane addressed?

3. Lane said, "Our strengths overused become our weaknesses." In what ways is this true for you?

4. What areas of personal development have gone unaddressed for too long in your own life?

5. What process do you have in place to help you address these development areas?

Letters

In an age like ours, which is not given to letter-writing,
we forget what an important part it used to play in people's lives.
—Anatole Broyard

Dear Lane,   5/12/95
It's been a few years since we've been in touch, but I felt the need to reach out to you because you were so helpful to me back when my dad was sick. Everything in my life is, once again, completely upside down. In the past couple months, I've gotten divorced from my husband, Britt, and quit my job at the Detroit Free Press.

I never expected to be divorced by my early twenties, and it's left me feeling totally defeated. Why didn't I date him for longer before I married him? Then I would've realized we each had very different goals. His charm captivated me. He was so doting and fun, and he provided rescue from the grief of losing my dad. But after I pulled myself together, I realized I had very little respect for his approach to life.

It seemed I was the only one keeping us grounded. All Britt wanted to do was spend money. He wanted to buy a house on the lake. He wanted a boat. He begged me to quit my job so my schedule would be more flexible for travel. He wanted to live this extravagant, rich, and famous life, and that just isn't me. He even had my mom ganging up on me about it! His tight relationship with my mom should have been another red flag! They were always worried about prestige, talking about what events we should be seen attending. That's just not me!

I didn't really want my life to change at all after receiving my dad's money. Sure, it's nice to know it's there, but I mostly ignore it so it doesn't destroy me or the things that are most important to me. Hmmm...I guess that might be happening anyway.

Britt says I'm hiding from the money, that I'm wasting it because I live like it doesn't exist. He says, "What's the use of having all the money your dad worked so hard for if you're not willing to enjoy it?"

In some ways, I guess he's right. I worry so much about everything. If I spent money on something extravagant with the inheritance, instead of the income I make from my job, I would feel like the stereotypical spoiled, obnoxious heiress. On the other hand, I'm tired of spending my life proving, to myself and everyone else, that I am not the typical trust-fund baby that everyone loves to hate. The blessing of this inheritance, the result of my dad's hard work and ingenuity...why does it feel like a dirty secret?

I love it when I meet people who know nothing about me. They have no preconceived notions about who I am. Do you know that when I applied for my job at the paper, the guy interviewing me actually asked me, "Why do you want a job? Didn't you just get a huge inheritance? You don't really need to work, right?" I never felt respected there because they all knew who I was, and they were always placating me, not taking me seriously, so I quit.

I'm already looking for another job. Each month, the investment office sends $2,500 of my dad's money over to my local bank account, so between that and my own money I've saved, I have several months to look for a good job before I run out of money. The thought of pulling more money out of the trust seems irresponsible.

Britt really wanted to take a trip to Europe. Since we couldn't afford it on our own income, I fought the idea. After we separated, I won a raffle at a local charity function. Guess what the prize was? A two-week European tour! Talk about sacred serendipity! I know you said that when coincidence strikes so strong in our lives, we should take note of what lesson we can learn from it. I haven't determined what that lesson is yet, but I leave next week, so maybe I'll have some insight while traveling around Europe.

I hope all is well with you, Lane.

In Transition,

Campbell ~~Newberry~~ Hannigan

Dear Campbell, 5/20/95

What a pleasure to receive correspondence from you. My sincere condolences on the death of your marriage to Britt. The death of a marriage requires a grieving process just like any other loss.

It also appears that your inheritance caused some problems in your marriage, which is not altogether uncommon. It may be likely that you're struggling, even within yourself, to make sense of the role that the inheritance plays in your life. Some inheritors face a struggle one author in my field calls "avoiding acculturation to wealth," which is a denial, and sometimes even a disdain, of your affluence.[1] To use a metaphor, it's a bit like moving to a new country but then resisting to adapt to the new culture. Perhaps this could be what's lurking beneath your current struggle? And if so, I wonder if there is a way to let bits of the new culture settle in while still holding onto the core values of your old self.

Regarding your work, listen to your heart as you choose your next steps. It benefits inheritors to choose purposeful work, a job that utilizes both your strengths and your passions. I'm certain you'll find a way to use this difficult time to propel you forward, as you have done with past hardships.

Lastly, I was hesitant to share this bit, but it may serve you well to know that your father never liked the old chap anyway. He used a word I hadn't yet encountered in American English to describe Britt. I believe your father called him a "shyster?"

Cheers,

Lane

Dear Lane,   6/9/95

Thank you so much for writing back. Your letter and the experience I had in Europe were surprisingly serendipitous. The feedback contained in your letter, which I opened and read on the day I returned from my trip, aligned perfectly with the insights I gained during my travels.

Do you recall that when my dad was in the hospital, I was reading Søren Kierkegaard's most famous writings for my philosophy class? You told me it was a coincidence because he and I shared a similar life story. Well, on my tour last week, we traveled through Copenhagen, Kierkegaard's hometown. When I walked up and saw a statue of him, I got goosebumps because I knew I was about to have some really important insights.

Did you know that he basically lived off his inheritance his whole life? He didn't make much money writing and pondering philosophy, but he certainly did make an impact on the world! This lightbulb went off in my mind; maybe there's a middle ground between Kierkegaard living completely off his inheritance and me treating mine like a hot potato!

At lunch that afternoon, I found, crumpled at the bottom of my backpack, a worn notecard. I wrote a Kierkegaard quote on that notecard right after our very first meeting together in the hospital. It read, "The most common form of despair is not being who you are."[2] The quote stood out to me that day. Somehow I knew it was important, so I wrote it down, but I couldn't find a way to make it fit. That notecard has been sitting in a small pocket of my bag unnoticed for years! In Copenhagen, I found it, and it fit like that lost piece of the puzzle you just knew you'd eventually find and squeeze right into its proper place.

I really have been in despair over the past couple of years. I figured it was just grief over losing my dad, but now I realize there's more to it. I've largely been pretending the wealth I inherited doesn't exist. I've been hiding from my deep passion, the thing I feel like I was born to do, because I worried that I couldn't make money doing it. I worry no one will want to publish my books, and I'll make no money. I worry people will see me as this annoying clichéd heiress who spends all her time pretending to work at "hobbies" like golfing, painting, or writing.

At the Royal Library garden in Copenhagen, I set down all those worries and left them there. I bought a notebook, sat down, and started writing my first novel. It's a story that has been in my heart since I was a teenager, and it felt so good to start putting it on paper. It's a novel for middle-school aged children, and its theme is, of course, the importance of being who you are. I couldn't be more energized about it, and I'm enjoying being free of the handcuffs I had placed on myself regarding my inheritance.

Now, you know me; I won't be driving around in a Ferrari or buying some over-the-top lakefront mansion, but I feel okay with utilizing my inheritance to help me pursue my purpose and passion in life.

The words of wisdom you shared in your letter confirmed all that I experienced on my trip. It wouldn't take a detective to notice that every time a giant lightbulb suddenly turns on above my head, the fingerprints of Lane Brock are everywhere!

Finally, I can't help but wonder about these moments of sacred serendipity. They are just too well-coordinated, too timely, too meaningful. Whoever is in charge of orchestrating them is thoughtful, poetic, and wise. I think this may be something worth exploring, and if you have thoughts on this, I would welcome your wisdom.

Best,
Campbell

YOUR MEETING WITH LANE

The Kierkegaard quote that keeps haunting Campbell reads, "The most common form of despair is not being who you are."

1. Think of a person (maybe yourself at some point in your life) who has struggled with despair. In what way were those feelings related to not being who you are?

2. Why might having substantial wealth make some people more susceptible to feeling despair?

3. What causes some people to feel a sense of guilt, shame, or denial about their wealth, especially when it is inherited?

4. What expectations, within society or within your own mind, exist about how those with inherited wealth should handle their finances? How much should a person depend on family wealth versus earned income to cover their expenses?

5. Campbell and her first husband, Britt, had different perspectives about the purpose and use of Campbell's inherited wealth. Is this a manageable problem, or must it always end in divorce? How can individuals in a marriage get on the same page about their wealth?

Late 1995

The Next Generation

Life affords no greater responsibility, no greater privilege,
than the raising of the next generation.
—*C. Everett Koop*

"I am head-over-heels in love with this boy! Tyler Hannigan, you are just the cutest baby I have ever seen in my life! Cole, don't you think he has Dad's eyes?"

Cole walked over to look at his newborn while tying his tie. "I don't know. I sort of think he looks like your baby pictures actually."

"Really? Wait, you're leaving? You can't leave me alone here with Tyler and your sketchy wife! Why can't you just take a morning off of work to hang out with your sister and your adorable newborn baby boy?"

"I missed a lot of work the last two days being in the hospital with Tyler, so I've gotta go in today. Listen, Lynne is the mother of my child now, so you have to be nice to her. Bye, Tyler. Be a good boy for your Auntie Campbell." Cole kissed the baby's wrinkled right foot.

Campbell lowered her voice to a whisper. "You know I don't trust her, Cole. I feel like this 'accidental' pregnancy was just her staking a claim to your money, and you know I wasn't happy when she guilted you into a quickie wedding just because she was pregnant. I'll stop bugging you to get a DNA test now, only because this child's adorable face screams Hannigan, but I will always be convinced that she's far more interested in the Hannigan fortune than in you."

Sliding his arms into the coat of his sharply-tailored, navy-blue suit, Cole admitted, "Well, you probably won't have to worry about Lynne anyway because she's spent most of her time in the guest room sleeping since we got home from the hospital. She didn't even wake up to feed Tyler last night, so I got up with him. I think she might be overdoing it on the pain pills they gave her, which has been a problem for her in the past."

Campbell glanced over at the bottle of pills sitting on the nightstand and picked it up, reading the label. "This says Modafinil. Are these her pills?"

"No. Those are mine. I don't sleep well, so the doctor prescribed them to help me stay alert through the day. Anyway, that's why I needed you to come over this morning, because I don't trust Lynne to stay awake to take care of Tyler. There's plenty of formula in the fridge, so you should be all set. Thanks so much for coming over, Campbell. You're the best." Cole grabbed the bottle of pills from Campbell's hand, shoved them in his pocket, and then he was gone—off to work at Hannigan Industries, warding off the demons that plagued him, his fears that he would become one of those horrible statistics. After Jim died, Lane Brock had tried again to motivate Cole's interest in her consulting process by sharing statistics about second- and third-generation family businesses.

"Cole, are you aware that less than one-third of all family-owned businesses survive the transition to the second generation?"[1]

Her words always echoed in his mind. Lane hoped these facts would serve as a wake-up call for Cole. She had wanted him to develop a board of directors for the business, which would have included some of the key executives at the company as well as his sister Campbell. Cole had said it would just confuse business practices. Before his death, Jim had asked Cole to go through the leadership development program Lane recommended. Cole had said he didn't have the time, and his dad seemed to understand. Lane had hoped to inspire and engage Cole, but her efforts just drove him deeper into his anxiety about maintaining the success of the business. This anxiety drove his intense partying on the weekend. This partying had led to a series of late-night rendezvous with several women, but most frequently Lynne, who had worked as a waitress at the dive bar one block from Hannigan Industries. These rendezvous with Lynne had led to Tyler. And now, the idea of having to raise Tyler with an unstable mother was leading to much more anxiety. Cole knew what it was like to have an unstable mother, and he deeply regretted handing down the same fate to his own son.

Lynne was proving to be unreliable, and Cole was in no position to raise a child on his own. He had a business to run, but he couldn't leave his son in Lynne's neglectful hands. He asked himself what his father would do.

Arriving at his office, Cole pressed the button on his phone that rang Cynthia. "Hey, I need you to look into hiring a full-time nanny for Tyler. Five days a week, twelve hour days. I need to hire someone as soon as possible. Looks like Lynne isn't going to be able to pull it together."

"I'll get started on it right away, sir. Shall I interview the prospects, or would you like to?"

Cole drummed his fingers nervously on the desk. "Actually, give Campbell a call and see if she'd be willing to do it. Just give her a list of three or four good prospects, and then she can interview them. Tell her I appreciate her help."

"Will do."

It had seemed like a great plan until he heard Campbell's voice on the other end of the phone early that afternoon.

"Am I your employee, or am I your sister?"

"What? What are you talking about?"

"First you dupe me into watching your newborn baby all day, and then you couldn't even call me to ask if I would interview nannies for Tyler? You had to have Cynthia call to ask me? This isn't work, Cole, this is family! Don't you understand the difference? Yes, I will help you hire a nanny, but only because I want someone amazing to care for this sweet baby who has been a perfect angel for me all morning while your sketchy wife smokes and watches game shows on TV in the guest suite. She hasn't even come out to check on him, not once!"

"Yeah, I know. She's a mess."

"I don't know what you were thinking, but you managed to find, impregnate, and marry a much darker version of Mom. You need to call your lawyer right now. You should take Lynne to court for full custody and kick her out of here ASAP."

"I know. I know. You're right. I hoped after she had Tyler

she would grow up, but I don't think that's going to happen."

"Well, I'll handle the nanny interviews, but you better arrange another babysitter until we find permanent help. I have a meeting with my publisher at the end of the week and I still have a ton of work to do on my book before then. Today, however, I am focused only on being Aunt Campbell. Do you care if I take Tyler over to my house for the rest of the day? Then you can come get him after work? He really shouldn't be in the house with her smoking."

"That would be great, Campbell. Thanks. You're the best."

"But please make sure you pick him up by six o'clock. I've got a date tonight with this handsome, very normal guy named Russ. He's from Florida and here on business for a few weeks. He already knows that I'm divorced, so if he comes to pick me up and I've got a newborn baby in my arms, there's no way I'll get a second date out of him."

"I'll be there on time, I promise."

Just over an hour before Cole's six o'clock pick up time, Campbell opened her front door to find three uniformed police officers asking if she knew anything about the where-abouts of "Lynne Hannigan's son, Tyler."

She looked down into her nephew's perfect newborn eyes and saw the myriad of challenges he would face in his future.

"I'm Tyler's aunt, Campbell Hannigan, and I'm not hand-ing Tyler over to anyone until my brother gets here."

YOUR MEETING WITH LANE

1. Jim and Cole's succession planning wasn't as extensive as it should have been. What factors keep business owners from developing a strategic business succession plan?

2. Cole resisted the idea of developing a board of directors. Why might this have been a good idea for Cole and for the business?

3. Who sits on the board of directors of your personal life? What friends and colleagues bring out the best in you and can be trusted to provide you with honest feedback? How can you better utilize this resource team in your life?

4. Campbell was hurt when Cole delegated the task of asking Campbell to interview nannies for Tyler, instead of calling to ask her directly. What was hurtful about this choice? In what ways do you bring a deeper level of intimacy to family or friendship relationships, distinguishing them from business relationships?

5. What is your family's marriage legacy? Many people with divorce in their family find that although they have a strong determination to avoid divorce, they lack the relationship skills to keep their marriage healthy. If there is a history of divorce in your family, how are you working to build your relationship skills?

1993

Tornado

I am a kite in a tornado, but I have a long string.
There is tension in my line.
Somewhere, someone is holding onto the other end and,
although it cannot spare me this storm,
it will not let me be lost while I regain my strength. It is enough.
— *Karen Marie Moning*

"Well, hello, everybody!"

Campbell, facing the window from her seat at the end of the hospital bed, turned from her conversation with her father and looked over her shoulder. Her mother, Debbie, tore into the hospital room like a tornado with no warning. Her jovial attitude seemed as inappropriate as her too-tight, too-short, gold skirt. Her hairstyle hadn't left the 1980s, with its bleached-blonde color and outrageous volume.

Debbie walked over to Jim's bedside and gave him a kiss on the cheek. "I've been just devastated about this, Jimbo. I cannot believe it. This cancer deal is getting just terrifying. Seems like everyone's got it! Did you hear my cousin Sandra has stage four breast cancer? She's in the middle of chemo and is just miserable. Oh, Jimbo, I hate to see you here in the hospital like this. You look good, though, honey. How do you feel?"

"I feel okay, actually. It's certainly a surprise to see you here. How long are you in town?"

"Oh, I can be here as long as you and Campbell need me to be here. I'm staying with the Newberry family. Do you remember that family from school, Cam?"

"Britt Newberry?" she answered too quickly, her stomach sinking.

"Yes, exactly! You remember his mother and I used to do that art class eons ago? Well, we reconnected, and she came to visit me in Chicago. We hit all the art museums, and we just had a blast together. When she heard about your father's illness, she called me and invited me to stay with them as long as I want. What a jewel she is! Have you ever met her, Cam? I know you and the son had a short little fling, but that never panned out, did it? What a shame. He's grown into such a handsome boy."

"When did you get into town, Mom?"

"Just last night, and boy am I exhausted! My plane was delayed, and my luggage took a full hour to come off the plane, so I didn't hit the pillow until 2 a.m. I'm way too old to go to bed that late. Look at these awful bags under my eyes!"

"Well, let's go get some coffee then, Mom. Dad, you've got your meeting with Lane soon anyway, right?"

"Who's Lane?" Debbie inquired.

Jim agreed, ignoring his ex-wife's prodding, "Yes, you two go and get some breakfast."

"See you soon," Campbell said, dropping her lips to her

father's forehead, which was getting dry and scaly from the radiation treatments. As she pulled back, she and her father exchanged a glance that spoke volumes of caution and concern about Debbie's arrival.

Campbell was usually able to speak up for herself, but her mother always made her stomach tie in knots and her thoughts jumble in her mind. As they both forced down rubbery cafeteria scrambled eggs, Campbell planned her words, emboldened by her concern for her family during this difficult time.

"Mom, I feel like it's a little awkward that you just showed up here unannounced."

Debbie picked up her napkin from her lap and dabbed the corners of her lips, stained with bright-pink lipstick. "Well, if I'm not wanted, then I guess I'll just…"

"Don't be like that. I'm just saying we weren't expecting you. It makes things uncomfortable. Cole will be around a lot. You know how he feels about you, and the last thing he needs is an unexpected run-in with you. He's very stressed with the business and worrying about Dad."

"Honey, you're forgetting that this is hard for me too. Your father and I had a very strong bond for many years, and I just had to see him. Of course, I had hoped to be here for you too. You're so young to be losing your father."

"But it's going to make things harder, not easier, to have you here in the middle of everything."

"Oh! Well, I see." Debbie's eyes welled up with tears. "I'm sure you're just feeling emotional, so I'm going to leave now. Mrs. Newberry and I are attending a charity gala tonight, and I'll never make it through the event if I don't get some rest. If you decide you'd like to see me while I'm here, you know where to find me. If not, well then I guess I'll know where we stand."

As Debbie marched off, Campbell's stomach churned. Why? Why did her mother always have to make everything harder? She couldn't let her do this again. Not now.

Of all the places her mother could stay—the Newberry house? Her time with Britt the other night had been perfect. Every time she'd thought about it, a jolt of excitement waved through her body. Her time with him had been a ray of sunshine in the midst of her stormy life. They had walked along Lakeshore Drive hand-in-hand, just talking, catching up. He had listened as she poured out her worries and fears. It crossed her mind that perhaps she had shared too much with him, especially now that she had learned about his family's connection to her mother.

Call him. She had to call Britt.

"Hello?" his very groggy voice came over the phone line.

"I'm sorry, Britt. Were you sleeping?"

"Campbell? What time is it?"

"It's 9 a.m."

"What's going on? Is everything okay?"

Campbell suddenly felt silly, like she had overreacted. "Yeah. Everything's okay. I'm sorry to wake you. I'm just stressing because my mom is in town, and I guess she's staying at your house? Did you know about all of this?"

"What? No, I just woke up. I mean, I guess that's obvious. Your mom is at my house? Right now? I'm so confused. I'm sorry, I feel like you're mad at me or something. Ugh. Can I get some coffee and maybe talk to my mom and call you back?"

"No. I mean, I'm at the hospital all day so you can't call me back. Britt, does your mom know that you and I went out together the other night?"

"No."

"Okay, good. Maybe don't tell her, or them. Our moms, I mean."

"Yeah, okay. I won't."

"And the charity ball that you invited me to tonight? I can't go. Apparently your mom invited my mom, so that's just not going to work."

"Okay. Look, Campbell, I didn't know about any of this. Can I meet you up at the hospital for lunch or something? We can talk all of this out?"

"Sure. Come at 12:30. Listen, I'm sorry to wake you like this. My mom, she just comes in and leaves a path of destruction behind her, so maybe just try to keep your distance, okay?"

"Yeah, okay, I will."

Campbell hung up the pay phone and walked around the corner to find Lane standing in front of the elevator.

"Good morning, Campbell."

Campbell struggled to put aside the stress of the morning. "Oh! Good morning. Aren't you supposed to be meeting with my dad right now?"

"We met for a bit, and then they came to get him for radiation. Schedule change, I guess. He asked me to find you and let you know you're needed for a meeting with the hospice team at 10 a.m."

"Hospice? Isn't that the group of nurses that comes in right before someone dies?" Campbell worried.

The two stepped into an alcove resembling a small living room adjacent to the busy elevator area as Lane offered reassurance. "No cause for alarm. Hospice undoubtedly does their best work with terminally-ill patients in those last days, but their team will also provide a range of services for your father and your family from this point forward. They'd like to explain their services, help you get connected to other resources, and answer any questions you may have. I'm glad to attend the meeting with you if you like, so you don't have to attend alone. I understand that you've already had a rather challenging morning."

"You could say that, yeah!" Campbell said, exhaling.

"Your father told me you had a rather unexpected visitor."

"My mother seems to have a gift for making everything more difficult."

"How does her presence here impact your handling of things?"

"Well, it adds stress, that's for sure. This morning after she arrived we ate breakfast together, and I tried to gently tell her that we don't want her here. Her presence here just makes it harder for everyone."

"It sounds like you were respectful but assertive with her. How did that feel, being assertive with your mother?"

"It was hard, and sad, and uncomfortable. But I would have exploded if I didn't say something to her."

Lane sat down in one of the cushy chairs, motioning for Campbell to do the same. "How did she respond to your assertiveness?"

"She cried and stormed off."

"Some people do have trouble hearing the word no, don't they?"

"Yeah. That's my mom!"

"How have you managed to handle having such a challenging mother, Campbell?"

Campbell laughed to herself and then answered, "Well, I've always had trouble standing up to her. The problem is, the older I get, the more I realize how unhealthy she is, and the stronger my convictions become, so I can't really keep my mouth shut. In this situation, I absolutely cannot handle having her make things any harder. I had to handle the situation for my dad's sake, for everyone's sake! I was respectful, so I'm trying not to feel bad about it, but my mother is the queen of the guilt trip!"

"You said the problem is that as you've gotten older, you've learned healthy boundaries and have gained a stronger sense of your convictions. That doesn't sound like a problem to me! It sounds like you're finding your voice and learning a strong sense of self-awareness."

"Well, I'm not so sure that I'm self-aware. My dad told me the dollar amount that I'll inherit when he dies. It shocked me. I didn't know—I had no idea. That's not very self-aware!"

"In what way does this number change who you are?"

Campbell sat quietly in thought for a full minute. "It doesn't. It doesn't change me at all."

"Not at all?"

"No. I would throw that money down to the streets of Detroit before I would allow it to ruin me."

Lane's eyes widened with surprise and then softened. "Well, that would certainly draw a crowd, wouldn't it? You believe that this degree of wealth has the potential to ruin your life?"

"Money makes people entitled. Snobby. Lazy. They spend money on extravagant clothes and jewelry and cars without a single thought of how far that money could go to help a sick child or a poor family."

"Where have you seen this dynamic of money ruining people in your life?"

"With some of my dad's customers. We'd go to these events at their houses or their country clubs like weddings, bar mitzvahs, or graduation parties. Everything was so over-the-top. It's like they all try to impress and outspend one another, but none of them seem happy. It's ironic, but they all seem so unfulfilled. They have everything you could ever want, but there's still such desperation in the way they live their lives. I can't stand the thought of being one of those people."

"Is it their money or their handling of the money that concerns you?"

Campbell stared at the opening and closing of the automatic doors at the hospital entrance, her mind bent in cognitive dissonance. "I guess it's their handling of the money that bothers me."

"Could a person have a substantial amount of money but handle it with values you deem admirable?"

"I think so. I'm thinking of my dad's lawyer. My dad told me one time that he really respects his lawyer because even though he has a ton of money, he lives a quiet, respectable life. He teaches an ethics class at the University of Michigan Law School. It's his faith, I think, that keeps him grounded; he's always at church or volunteering. He's a great lawyer and extremely successful, but he and his family are completely down-to-earth, normal people."

"So a person could be wealthy without their wealth becoming the center of their lives, without it ruining them?"

"I hope so."

Lane leaned in toward Campbell, putting her elbows on her knees, and looked directly into her eyes. "Campbell, make no mistake, fifty million dollars will change your life in many ways, some that you cannot control. I know you'd prefer to avoid it all and keep life unchanged, but that's not today's reality. The challenges of inheriting wealth go well beyond temptations to max out your credit cards and drink too many chocolate martinis. Your inheritance will impact every aspect of your life: your career choices, where you choose to live, how you choose to spend your free time, how you raise your children, who you choose to marry. It will impact every close relationship. Some relationships will be able to handle this pressure, and some will not. The good news is that you are not facing these challenges alone. I am here to help you accept your inheritance, embrace the notion of yourself as an inheritor, and set goals for a future of handling all of it in a way that would make you, and your father, very proud."

Standing up from the brown leather chair, Campbell turned her back to Lane and walked a few paces to the window overlooking the busy front circle of the hospital. The commotion of the scene echoed the upheaval going on inside of her. Silence filled the air between them as Campbell wrestled with this new understanding of herself and her future. Thoughts buzzed around like hurried cars in her mind.

"The most common form of despair is not being who you are. Who am I? Who will I become?"

Campbell turned around to Lane, eyes filling with tears and fixed on the floor. "I don't know or understand the

Campbell on the other side of my dad's death. The Campbell without Jim Hannigan, but with fifty million dollars, is a total stranger to me. I'm not smart enough to manage that kind of money. Cole got the As. Cole went to business school. He gets all of this. I don't."

"You don't get it. You don't know. You don't understand. You aren't smart enough. These are your fears talking, Campbell, because I've not seen even a smidgen of evidence to suggest you can't handle what's required of you. You are self-aware. Strong values are at the core of your identity. You desire to learn and grow, ready to do whatever it takes to properly handle life's challenges. These important qualities will be a cornerstone of strength for you. Your results on the emotional intelligence assessment you completed for me last time show a few small areas for growth, but overall indicate that you're quite balanced, mature, and capable."

Lane reached into her briefcase and pulled out a copy of the book *Emotional Intelligence* by Daniel Goleman.[1]

"Have you seen this book? It's on the bestseller list and completely revolutionizes how we understand intelligence. The author would argue that your strengths are precisely the kind of intelligence that predicts success. Go ahead, take my copy and read it. And here's a copy of your assessment results."

"Thank you." Campbell walked over to Lane, took the book, and skimmed its back cover, making her way back over to the window.

"We can discuss the assessment in further detail at our meeting tomorrow. For now, I have just one more question for you, Campbell. On a scale of one to ten, where one is low and ten is high, how confident are you that the woman you are today has the ability to handle her father's death, her inheritance, and her future with her values intact?"

This question seemed to shift Campbell's perspective. As she stared out the window, a hollow formed in her heart. She grieved the loss of innocence, of simplicity in her life, and accepted her complicated future. Things would never be easy again. Her carefree days were mostly behind her. She could become a woman capable of handling these challenges, or she could allow them to break her. Slowly, emerging from inside her, she felt a surge of confidence. For the first time in her life, she set down the image of herself as a naive child and imagined herself as a confident, capable woman. The tornado of emotion about her mother's intrusion, about all that she was losing in her father, about all that was changing in her life settled, and the scattered pieces of her life landed more solidly into place.

After a long silence, Campbell turned from the window toward Lane, and with steely resolve replied, "Nine."

"Nine?"

"I'm a nine."

Lane shot Campbell a wink. She cupped her hand to the side of her mouth as if to pronounce to a crowd, "Look out, world. It looks like young Hannigan has finally found her moxie!"

Campbell laughed and felt the tension release from her neck. The often-serious Lane let out a small chuckle. "Yes, let's get a good laugh in now before the hospice team ruins our day entirely."

Campbell leaned into her new sense of resolve during the meeting with the hospice staff. She managed the overwhelming details like a student in a college classroom, taking notes and asking questions regarding insurance, medica-tions, medical equipment, and home care. The meeting turned surreal when the nurse shared in detail the expected course of her father's illness and impending death. It was still so hard for her to believe that it was her father they were talking about—that it was his body that would be shutting down. She expected to feel crippled by the fear of facing her caregiving role, but she found herself feeling ready for the fight. She wanted to do it for her dad. For all he had given to her, she was glad she could give something back.

YOUR MEETING WITH LANE

1. What person in your life challenges your ability to exercise healthy boundaries? How can you improve your skills at appropriately setting healthy boundaries with the difficult people in your life?

2. Lane asked Campbell if a person could be wealthy without wealth being the center of their lives. What do you think?

3. What is it about wealth that has the potential to "ruin" people as Campbell described?

4. How can wealthy people avoid allowing their wealth to define them and their values?

5. What insights did Campbell have that increased her resolve to handle the challenges she faced?

1993

A Tough Pill to Swallow

Everybody knows they're going to die, but nobody believes it.
If we did we would do things differently".
—*Mitch Albom,* Tuesdays with Morrie

"Daddy, you remember Britt Newberry, right?"

"Of course. Hello, Britt. Good to see you again."

"Hello, Mr. Hannigan. It's great to see you again too. Listen, I'm so sorry to hear about . . . Campbell told me... your diagnosis. I'm very sorry." Campbell blushed at her date's awkward fumbling.

"Thank you, Britt. I appreciate that you're getting Campbell out for a few hours and away from the stress of caring for her old man. That week in the hospital was brutal for both of us, and we're happy to be home this week, seeing the light of day."

Campbell interrupted, "Oh! Britt and I were just planning to stay here and watch a movie or play darts in the basement. Your meds are due at 8:30 tonight, and I know you have a lot of trouble swallowing that big pill."

"Nonsense, Cammie. I'm a big boy; I can swallow my pills without you hovering over my shoulder. Anyway, Lane is coming over at seven o'clock for our next meeting, so I'm sure she can deliver the Heimlich maneuver if it becomes tragically necessary."

Laughing, Campbell replied, "Okay, well, I'm warming these mashed potatoes for you to eat for dinner. Is that still what sounds good to you?"

"That sounds delicious, dear, thank you," Jim said warmly and motioned for Britt to follow him out to the living room. "So tell me, Britt, what's been keeping you busy these days?"

"Well, I've been working a lot, and when I'm not working, I try to get out to the garage to work on my dad's '67 Corvette."

"Really! I bet she's a real beauty. Have you got her running yet?"

"No, not just yet, but soon, hopefully."

"Well, I'm glad to hear you're working hard. You know what I always tell Campbell and her brother, 'There's nothing more important than—'"

"—working hard at work worth doing," Campbell yelled from the kitchen, finishing her father's sentence.

"That's right." Jim smiled with pride. "I've said it before, and I'll continue to say it. We're all born with talent, and we've gotta put it to work! What kind of work has had you so busy lately, Britt?

"Well, a couple of buddies and I are working on this startup. It's an internet business, but I've also been working at Home Depot until the business gets going."

Jim got himself settled onto the brown leather couch in the middle of the great room, with its cathedral ceilings and dark wood floors. "I'm ashamed to admit that I'm not as tech-savvy as I'd like to be, so I may regret asking, but I'd love to know more about the work you're doing with your new computer company."

Britt sat in the armchair next to Jim, unconsciously picking his fingernails while he spoke. "It's a website where you can chat with friends or share updates."

Jim waited for Britt to share more but then found a kind reply. "I see. It seems that the internet is really taking off. My broker is trying to get me to invest in some of these 'dot-com' stocks," he said, making air-quotes. "I told him, give it four more years, and then he can get me invested into all these internet businesses. It's such a new industry, and the valuation of these companies seems a little shaky to me. I mean, what's their tangible product? Campbell, did you hear that, dear? You tell those brokers not to get you invested in those tech stocks just yet, okay?"

"O-kay?" Campbell replied from the kitchen.

Jim continued, now focused back on Britt. "It takes a tenacious entrepreneurial spirit to get a new business off the ground. Tell me about your business team."

"It's just a couple of guys from around here. My one friend, his degree is in computer science, so he's the tech side of things. My other buddy is doing the accounting, and my degree is in marketing, so..."

"How are things progressing in the marketing department? Are you making some good contacts in your field? So much of doing good business these days is networking."

"I've mostly been working on the branding side of things up to this point. We're still trying to break into some good contacts."

"I see. Well, it sounds like my work may be very different from yours, but if there's anything I can do, don't hesitate to ask."

"Yeah. Thanks. I think we are all set for now, but thank you, Mr. Hannigan."

Campbell placed the bowl of mashed potatoes, along with a cup of hot tea, on the table in front of Jim.

"Thank you. That smells wonderful." Jim eyeballed the whiskey decanter sitting atop the small bar across the living room and thought it would make a nice addition to his tea. As he stood, Jim quickly grabbed his hip, a sharp pain bolting down his leg. He winced in pain and dropped back down onto the couch. Reading his thoughts, Campbell grabbed the decanter and brought it to Jim. Britt's eyes met hers with a worried glance as Jim continued to rub his pained hip.

Sipping his hot toddy, Jim waved off their concerns. "Alright, you kids go on now and have a good time tonight."

"I think the cancer has moved into his hip," Campbell whispered and pushed her lower lip out into a sad face as they dropped down into the seats of Britt's car. He leaned across the seat and dropped a small, comforting kiss, their first, onto her lips. Pulling back, he smiled at her. "You're one tough cookie, you know that?"

Campbell received the kiss and his encouragement gladly, but she still had some reservations about Britt's connection to her mother. "So, is my mom still squatting at your house?"

"Yeah, although I don't see her much because they're always out on the town. I think they're out to dinner tonight on a double date or something. I guess my dad had a single friend he brought along as a date for your mom."

"Really! I wonder if her used-car-salesman husband in Chicago is aware of that."

"Listen, I really hope this issue doesn't get in the way of what seems to be a good thing we have starting here, Campbell. I told you last week when we ate lunch together at the hospital, it doesn't matter to me who your parents are, your family drama or whatever. I just want to be with you. Let's forget all about them and get your mind off of all this stress. So, I heard there's a comedian downtown at the Fox Theater tonight. If we hurry, we'll get there right on time."

"I don't know, Britt. I'm dressed kind of casually. I hate to go too far in case my dad needs me. How long is the show?"

"If you don't take time to have some fun when you can, Campbell, you're going to burn out on this caregiving role." He leaned across the console, bringing his face very close to hers. "You are amazing, Campbell, the kind of girl that deserves to be wined and dined and treated like a princess. You're going through something really tough, and you'd better get used to being taken care of now that you're with me."

"Well, that sounds pretty incredible to me." Campbell smiled, running her finger underneath Britt's chin and then snapping back in her seat playfully. "All right, you're very convincing. Let's go, or we're going to be late!"

Britt pulled out of the driveway and made his way downtown. They laughed, and soon the weight of all the stress Campbell had been carrying felt a bit lighter. As they neared their exit off the highway, Britt lifted himself up off the driver's seat, yanking his wallet from his back pocket and flipping it open. "Shoot. Hey, you do have your purse with you, right? I wasn't planning on doing this tonight, so I'm not sure I have enough cash for the tickets. My credit card is maxed out from the marketing materials I just bought for the business, so I'm not sure I have enough money to cover us tonight."

"Oh, yeah, I have my purse. No worries."

Back at home, Jim startled awake at the sound of a loud rapping on the heavy mahogany front door. Between the radiation and medication, Jim, who was normally buzzing with energy, now seemed to constantly fight sleep.

"Sorry, Ms. Brock. I think I may have dozed off. Were you waiting out here on the porch for very long?"

"No. I knocked twice, but it's no trouble. And remember, I prefer to have you call me Lane."

"Yes. Lane. That's what Campbell calls you, so I suppose I should too."

"Yes. I've specifically requested that she call me Lane. It's important that she begin seeing me, and the other business professionals she will be working with, as peers. It can be a bit disempowering to discuss legal and financial matters while seated across the table from people who've seen you toddling around in diapers. Encouraging Campbell to address your lawyer and accountant by their first names can't erase those challenges, but is a subtle change that communicates volumes. You know, despite it all, I must say, it's quite a stalwart young girl you've got in that one."

Jim laughed. "If that means stubborn, then I agree!" He walked her into the living room and they each got settled, Jim back on the couch and Lane in an adjacent armchair.

"She's been quite motivated and fully invested in our sessions. She's determined to do well. I don't think you'll have to worry about her at all. Your son, on the other hand, is an entirely different story. He's been rather disengaged and distracted. Working around the clock. Saying he doesn't have time for some of the work I've recommended for him. Frankly, I'm concerned about Cole."

"Oh, that just sounds like typical Cole to me. He's always so driven, he never takes time for himself. Of course, if I'm honest, I'd rather have him distracted with work than getting himself into trouble. You know what they say about idle hands! Cole's never given me a bit of trouble. He'll dive neck-deep into the business, and that's what will keep him sane through all of this. I don't worry too much about Cole."

"With all due respect, Jim, I fear we may have opposing perspectives on your children and their capacity to handle this situation and the challenges they'll face in the future. I gave them each a social and emotional intelligence assessment. Have you heard of emotional intelligence? It's a rather new term."

"No, I'm sorry. I don't think I have," Jim replied, shifting his painful left hip off the couch. He noticed his crusty mashed potato bowl sitting on the coffee table and wished that he had taken it to the kitchen sink before Lane had arrived.

"I find that emotional intelligence is far more predictive of leadership effectiveness than education or IQ. This aptitude includes skills like innovation, integrity, resilience, conflict management, self-awareness, achievement drive, optimism, empathy, and other skills you may have heard termed 'soft skills.'"

"Oh, yes. Now that you describe it, I believe I read an article about this in the newspaper a while back. It caught my eye because of the significant increase in sales production of the group that participated in the emotional intelligence training."

"Yes. I'm so pleased you're familiar with these important outcomes because I think Hannigan Industries could benefit greatly, especially through this transition time, if Cole would participate in my leadership coaching process."

"Well, I'll talk to him about it."

"Thank you, Jim. I think your encouragement will really help. So tell me what thoughts you've been having about the topics we discussed during our last meeting."

"I've been writing on those cards—you know, the kinds of capital I'm investing in, financial, intellectual, social, human, and spiritual capital. And I also worked on finding the three words that people will remember me by."

"And what did you discover?" Lane pulled a notepad and a pen from her briefcase.

"Well, both tasks were very hard for me. I've never thought much about anything like that before. These tasks have made me think more about what I'm saying and doing in the time I have left. You know, I realized something. There was this art print in my hospital room of a beautiful sailboat on the water. Not sure if I ever mentioned that I have a sailboat and just love to take it out when I can. Out on the water is really the only place I can truly relax. Sailing is one of my true loves in this life, but I realized, I've never really shared it with my kids, and I don't know why. I mean, I took them out a couple of times, but I was usually out there alone or with customers or employees. I'm really regretting that I never really taught my kids how to sail. I regret that they didn't get to know that relaxed dad out on the water. I regret that they don't appreciate the humility you feel when you're out there sailing on the open water, dependent upon the wind, submissive to the waves. Why didn't I just take a few weekends and bring the kids out there with me?"

Lane watched Jim stare off into the distance. "What a coincidence, with your great love of sailing, that your particular hospital room would have this particular piece of artwork on the wall. I call surprising coincidences like this 'sacred serendipity.' This moment with the sailboat print in the hospital spoke to you somehow. What did it say?"

"It made me realize there are aspects of myself that I have kept from my kids. Some of what I keep from them might even be the best parts of me. There's something spiritual that awakens inside of me when I'm out on the water. I don't have much of anything to write on that spiritual capital card because I've never felt comfortable going there with my kids. How do you give words to something so personal? There's a prayer I say at night when I'm out on the water. It speaks to the reality that, try as we may, none of us control the wind and the waves. You know, I want my kids to be humble. I want them to know there's more to life than business, or wealth, or success. And I want them to find the space where they can relax and find that deep place in themselves to talk to God. But when I think about it, I've never shared any of that with them. In fact, all I've ever encouraged them to be is independent, strong, self-assured, and driven. Those values are extremely important, but they aren't the only things that are important. I can see it now. I just don't know why I couldn't see it before."

Lane didn't want to tread on the sacred space that Jim's deep words had created, so she waited a few moments and then reflected.

"Facing your death seems to be giving you a new perspective on life. You've spent your time focusing on passing down legacy values in the area of work ethic and achievement drive, but you're regretting not passing down your love of sailing and the humility and faith that sailing awakens inside of you. This is one of the most important parts of who you are, and you fear you've missed your chance to pass on those legacy values. Coming to this realization now, with so little time left, is a pretty tough pill to swallow."

Jim's eyes welled up with tears.

"You're not dead yet, Jim Hannigan," Lane said with a wink, leaning in toward him and catching his gaze. "Have you seen the weather forecast for this week? Starting Wednesday, they're predicting high temperatures in the low eighties. With weather this warm during late fall in Detroit, one has to wonder if the same God that controls your wind and waves also controls the temperature! Do you think you might be able to take the two kids out for a bit of sailing this week?"

A small hint of hope spread across Jim's face. "I guess I could. It would have to be Wednesday because the boat's scheduled to be put away for the winter on Thursday. I'm so sorry I never made sailing a family tradition we shared, but at least we may have the chance to make a memory together, I suppose. Maybe I can even teach them a thing or two about taking care of that gorgeous sailboat. Who knows, one of them may even want to hold onto the 'Motor City Sails' and learn how to sail her."

"Maybe, indeed. I wouldn't mind at all if you took a moment to contact the children now, to extend the invitation."

Lane excused herself to the restroom while Jim picked up the phone to call Cole. She returned to hear the final words of the message he left on Cole's answering machine.

"...So I hope to see you then. Should be a fun day. Goodbye, Cole."

As Lane sat back down, Jim explained that he'd wait until Campbell arrived back home to invite her on the sailing adventure.

"You know she's out with this boy, Britt Newberry, and I don't think I really like him."

"The same sentiment shared by all fathers of beautiful young women, I presume," Lane said, smiling.

"Ah, I'm sure," Jim replied politely, continuing, "but, really. This kid says he's working on some internet startup business, but he can hardly tell me a thing about it. He says he's the marketing exec, but he has no contacts and no interest in having me help him get connected. I'll tell you what I think: this 'startup,'" Jim made air quotes, "is just something to talk about when all the boys get together to have some beers. It's a pipe dream! He's wasting time working at Home Depot, and I'll bet his career won't ever amount to much more...unless, of course, he lands Campbell Hannigan, and then he can live life on easy street. She's just so naive; can't she see how vulnerable she is?"

Jim wished he could manage the pieces of his life like a chess game. Even after his death, he would love to be able to protect Campbell and Cole from harm and advance their chances of success. Unfortunately, it just wasn't that easy.

After all, he couldn't control the wind and the waves, and with his children now grown adults, he certainly couldn't control them. He'd share his opinion with Campbell about this boy, but it was up to her to make her own choices. Jim made a mental note to ask his lawyer if it was possible to make Campbell's distributions from his trust dependent upon her signing a prenuptial agreement when she married.

"Have you shared your concerns about this boy with Campbell?" Lane asked.

Jim pointed and bounced his index finger in the air. "No, but you can bet your bottom dollar that I will!"

"What might be the best approach in handling this sensitive issue?"

"Hmm. That's a good question. I should really spend more time thinking about this kind of thing. If I'm not careful, I might drive her right toward him. Seems that's the way it works with fathers and daughters, right?"

"In general, I find that parenting young adults is best approached by offering more questions than answers. They need space to think through their choices and approach handling situations independently. Offering questions opens the mind. Offering advice narrows the mind. And I'll bet by now your children know you so well they could predict your opinion on most situations without you having to speak a word! Ask Campbell what she thinks of Britt, what she thinks of his business, what she's looking for in a partner. Ask her how she'll know if a boy likes her or is just interested in her money. Ask her how she'll handle the power differential that money can create in relationships. Your questions will drive her to consider these questions and think through these situations that will be unique to her because of her wealth. Then, just listen, and ask more questions."

Jim tugged thoughtfully at his lower lip. "Well, that's a new approach for me, but I'm willing to give it a try."

After finishing up their remaining business, Jim walked Lane out to the foyer. He opened the door to find Debbie standing on the porch, ready to knock. All three looked at one another in surprise.

"Oh, I'm so sorry. I didn't realize you'd have a guest over in your condition, Jim." Debbie held her waist-length fur coat together with one hand to keep out the cold wind of the evening, and reached out her other hand to greet Lane.

"I'm Debbie...Jim's ex-wife."

Jim quickly stepped in. "Debbie, this is Ms. Brock. She's a consultant I've hired to help me pull my affairs together. We were just finishing up our meeting."

"Pleasure to meet you. What was your first name?"

Jim motioned for Lane to step outside, and shut the door to the house, heading out onto the porch with the two women. "I'm not really feeling up to a visit, Debbie, so why don't you just follow Ms. Brock out to the driveway."

"Well, I'm not here to visit you, Jim. I came by to spend some time with my daughter."

Lane questioned what to do, but chose to linger long enough to ensure Jim had the strength to defend himself from Debbie's persistence.

"Campbell isn't here. She's out with a friend tonight," Jim retorted.

"I know!" Debbie snickered. "That's why I stopped by! I can't wait to hear all about her date with that handsome Britt Newberry. His mother was kind enough to invite me to stay with them while I'm in town since I'm not welcome here. We were out to dinner tonight, and she mentioned that those two lovebirds seem to be making quite a love connection. Wouldn't that just be fantastic!"

"Well, you can give her a call tomorrow, but for now, you should call it a night, Debbie," Jim said, putting an arm around her and directing her toward the driveway.

The two women stood on the porch in stark contrast to one another, Lane a picture of class in business attire, standing next to Debbie in a tight skirt, gold heels, and fur coat. As the women walked out to their cars, Jim's blood began to boil. Why did Debbie always stir up trouble? He didn't have the energy for her drama right now. He continued to ponder her motives as he sat back down on the couch after watching Debbie's rental car drive away. Somehow, despite his angry swirl of thoughts, he must have drifted off, because the next thing he knew, Campbell was standing in front of him.

"You want to move into your bedroom, Daddy? You'll sleep better there."

He slowly opened his eyes and a big sleepy grin moved across his dry lips. "Hi, honey. How was your evening?"

"It was great! How was your meeting with Lane?"

"My meeting with Lane was great until your mother showed up unannounced."

"She didn't!"

"She did. And if you don't answer her calls tomorrow morning, you can bet she'll be over here again. Seems she's over the moon that you're dating Britt Newberry. What's that about?"

"I'm not totally sure, but don't worry. I'll call her tomorrow."

As the two traveled to the kitchen, Jim moved out of his fog of slumber and tried to remember what Lane had said about how to approach a conversation about Britt. "Well, what do you think of him?"

"Nailed it," Jim thought to himself.

Campbell giggled.

"What's so funny?" His confidence sank. Maybe he hadn't nailed it.

"I don't know! I've never talked to you about boys before!"

"So, what do you think of him?" Jim pressed on with a smile.

"He was really sweet to me. He's the kind of guy that holds doors open for you and makes you feel like a princess. At first, I didn't know what to think of all of that attention, but I think I could get used to it! He took me to a comedy show, and we laughed and had so much fun. It was just what I needed!"

Her words made Jim's head spin with worry, but he tried to stay on course. "Honey, have you thought about what qualities you're looking for in a long-term partner, or even a husband?"

"Geez! I had fun tonight, but not that much fun!"

"Well, sure, but generally speaking, have you thought about what characteristics you might want in a husband? It's important for you to think about this. God knows your mother and I didn't set a very good example for you and your brother. I never thought about what I wanted or needed. I just did what felt right at the moment. That wasn't the right approach for me, and I hope you'll learn from my mistakes and be more thoughtful about choosing who you'll spend the rest of your life with…especially in light of your inheritance. Money can make things, well, tricky." Jim recognized himself slipping into advice-giving mode and revised his approach as Lane suggested. He grabbed a piece of paper and pen from the table. "Here. You start listing traits, and I'll write them down."

"This seems like something I would have done in junior high at a sleepover with my girlfriends!" Campbell reluctantly played along. "Okay. Let me think." After a few moments she began. "Honesty. I cannot stand being lied to! I guess because of how Mom always lies to get her way. It drives me crazy. Honesty is super-important."

Jim wrote the first bullet point and looked back up at her. "Also, compassion. I want someone who has genuine concern for me but also for the world and people in general. Like tonight, Britt seemed genuinely concerned about you after we left. I like that."

Jim bit his tongue, snarling to himself. "Oh yeah. I'm sure that was completely genuine. He's playing you like a fiddle, my sweet girl."

"We've got honesty and compassion. What else? Give me two more," Jim requested.

"Also, passion. I want someone who loves life and won't sort of mope through every day, but will find purpose and live life to the fullest. On the other hand, I don't want someone too passionate because I need him to be stable and grounded, someone I can trust to make good choices. And finally, I want someone who is family-oriented. I want a husband who will make me, and maybe our kids, a top priority. The kind of husband who comes to soccer games and dance recitals, helps with the dishes, plans family vacations, and is always there at bedtime to tuck the kids in and kiss his wife goodnight."

Campbell got so carried away sharing the details of this dream for her future that she didn't see how her words stung Jim's ears. In them, he heard echoes of regrets about all the moments he had missed in his daughter's life as he worked to keep the business thriving.

Jim cleared his throat, trying to swallow the emotion her words had stirred in him. "Honesty, full of compassion, passionate yet grounded, and family-oriented. Here's your list." He handed her the list. As she looked down at it, she knew this list, with his characteristically neat handwriting, would become one of her most treasured possessions after he was gone.

"Wait, Daddy. There's still room at the bottom of the paper for two more. Now you add some." She slid the paper back across the counter in front of him.

"Well, as you know, I haven't had much luck in love. Lasting love, that is. I might not be the best one to ask."

"It's not about you. It's about what you want for me. What you think I need. When I'm deciding who I want to marry, you won't be around to share your opinion, so speak now or forever hold your peace."

Jim tried hard to push out painful images of his daughter's future wedding without him present. Forcing concentration, he tapped the end of the pen on his temple. "Okay then. Let me think. Humility. You want your husband to be humble."

"Really? I thought for sure you'd start with 'hardworking' or 'confident' or 'driven!'"

"See, I've still got some tricks up my sleeve, young lady. I'm seeing things a little differently lately, it seems. Humility is important. You want your partner in life to be humble. I've never talked with you about this, but I believe in my heart that there is a God who cares about our little lives, and leaving my life in his hands helps me stay humble. I think you'd do very well to have a husband who leads your future family with the same conviction."

"I guess I knew you believed in God, but I've never heard you talk about it like that. Okay, humility. Write it down. What else?"

"The last value I think your husband should have is devotion. Choose a man who is devoted to you, and only you, for life. Especially for you, with the money, you need someone who will love you for the amazing, smart, passionate, beautiful girl you are. The money will be appealing to guys because they may think it'll guarantee a life on easy street. They'll exploit you for it if you aren't careful. And Cammie, don't look for devotion in their eyes—their eyes will fool you every time. What guy wouldn't look into that gorgeous face with hearts in his eyes? You've got to look for it in how he behaves toward you every day. Does he respect your ideas? Does he make you his top priority? When you talk about the future, is his focus on you, or on your money? Is he patient with you? In what ways does he uphold your values, passions, and goals for the future? I want you to have a husband totally devoted to you, Cammie. That's what I want. That's what you deserve."

Jim wrote down these last two words, humble and devoted at the bottom of the paper as Campbell walked over and wrapped her arms around her father's shoulders.

"Thank you so much for that, Daddy."

"I'm sorry I'll miss your wedding. I bet you'll make the most beautiful bride."

"Oh, you'll be there, Daddy." She lifted the paper up and held it to her heart. "You must be exhausted. Let's get you to bed. You took your meds earlier while Lane was here, right?"

"Yes, dear, I took my meds. You're like a nurse now. Maybe you could be a nurse rather than a writer."

"What are you doing? We just had this beautiful moment!"

"Sorry, sorry. You're right. I should stop while I'm ahead. Hey, listen, I was thinking maybe we should go out on the sailboat together this Wednesday. You, Cole, and me. It's supposed to be beautiful weather."

YOUR MEETING WITH LANE

1. What aspects of yourself have you withheld from your children as Jim did with his faith and his love for sailing? What concerns motivated you to withhold these parts of yourself?

2. What aspects of your own parents' lives do you feel you were excluded from? What may have motivated them to hold these parts of themselves back?

3. Why is the decision of who a person marries so important? How does wealth complicate marriage?

4. How can you avoid the trap of feeling the need to lecture your children, and adjust your approach in conversations to help equip and empower them with more open-ended questions?

1999

Having It All

The trouble with being rich is that, since you can solve with your checkbook virtually all of the practical problems that bedevil ordinary people, you are left in your leisure with nothing but the great human problems to contend with: how to be happy, how to love and be loved, how to find meaning and purpose in your life.
—*Frederick Buechner*

"Well, this Saturday is my day, so don't you dare cause drama. You'll just have to find a way to be around her. I can't get married without Mom there, Cole." Campbell lounged in a cozy black leather chair, scolding her brother through the slatted dressing room door of the tuxedo shop.

Cole laughed. "You DID get married without Mom there—without anyone there, for that matter! Did you forget your name was Campbell Newberry for a couple of years?"

"Yeah, well, that's because Dad had just died the year before, and I couldn't handle the thought of getting married without him walking me down the aisle. You know, my strong urge to elope should've been my first indication that my marriage to Britt was not the right decision."

"Well, at least you only lost two years of your life and a couple hundred thousand dollars on your bad marriage. As much as I love Tyler, when you have a kid during your bad marriage, it becomes a never-ending nightmare." Still adjusting his bow tie, Cole opened the door and revealed himself to Campbell and the three-way mirror.

"Whoa. You look amazing!" Campbell admired.

He smiled and winked at his sister, running his fingers through his wavy blonde hair.

"Thanks!" he replied, checking his watch and moving back into the dressing room. "Okay, this is a good fit, right? I've gotta get back to work." Cole closed the door to the dressing room.

"No lunch?"

"No, sorry. I've got the guys from Enterprise coming in from Chicago for a meeting today."

"What's Enterprise? Like the rental car place?"

"No. Shoot, I thought I told you! Enterprise does the same kind of work as we do, but on a much larger scale. They have companies all over the Midwest. They've gotten into some financial trouble, and I'm considering buying them out, so all of Enterprise could become part of Hannigan Industries by the end of the year."

"No, you didn't tell me, Cole. That's a really big deal! Congratulations!" In her excitement, Campbell burst into the unlocked dressing room to find her brother in his T-shirt and boxer shorts, kneeling over the dressing room bench snorting a white powder.

"What the hell are you doing?" She rammed her brother's shoulder back against the wallpapered dressing room wall. Cole, shocked by Campbell's intrusion, allowed her physical affront but would not make eye contact with her.

"This is a big meeting, Campbell. I've got to be at my best, and I'm just not sleeping well lately." Cole mumbled.

Campbell slid the drugs onto the carpeted floor and whisper-yelled, "What is this, Cole, cocaine?"

"No! Relax! It's just speed."

"It's just speed? You think this crap is going to make you function at your best? Who are you? Dad would be mortified if he was still here and saw you doing this."

Cole rubbed the back of his hand across his nose and bent down to put on his pants, turning his back to Campbell. "Dad was an alcoholic, Campbell. Did you miss the fact that he drank scotch every single day? You don't get it. This business is cutthroat. If this acquisition falls through, I'm screwed. Detroit is sinking. The automotive industry is changing, and not for the better. And I've got nothing to fall back on. I literally lost millions of dollars in investments last year when the dot-com bubble burst. Millions of dollars! This is the real world. I guess we all find our ways of coping."

Campbell sat down on the bench, trying to absorb these realities. Her brother was snorting drugs. How deeply had he sunk into addiction? Had he really lost millions of dollars? Had her father really been an alcoholic? She admitted to herself that he drank nearly every day, but she'd never thought of him as an alcoholic. He was never an angry, sloppy drunk, and he functioned just fine. How could he have been an alcoholic and she never realized it?

Cole wrapped up the uncomfortable conversation as he finished tying his tie. "You're painfully naive, little sister, but that's why I love you. Don't worry about anything. Dad was fine. I'm fine. Mom and I will get along fine on Saturday at your wedding. I looked pretty darn fine in this tuxedo that

I'll be wearing to walk you down the aisle. And your wedding will be a most fantastically fine day. Go finish planning the details of your big day, and don't worry about me." He dropped a kiss on her cheek, grabbed his suit coat, and left her in the dressing room alone.

His condescension lit a fire inside her. Campbell pulled her phone from the back pocket of her jeans and impulsively dialed.

"Hello?" a young female voice answered.

"Jen. Hi, this is Campbell."

"Oh, hi, Campbell! I'm just at the park for a picnic lunch with Tyler before I take him to preschool. What's up?"

Campbell wasted no time. "I'm calling about my brother. I just saw him snorting drugs. Are you aware of this?"

Tyler's nanny hesitated. "I mean, it's not really my place to get involved. I sort of turn a blind eye to things like that that go on within my client families."

"Turn a blind eye? There is a child in the house! Cole must be doing this all the time if he's doing it in front of you. And Tyler—has Cole done drugs in front of Tyler?"

"No, of course not!"

"Listen to me. I know you would never dream of jeopardizing your posh nanny life, but if I find out that you have allowed Tyler to be endangered in any way by my brother's behavior, I will take you down. If anything happens to put my nephew at risk in any way, do you promise you will call me immediately?"

"Yes! Yes, I'll call you."

The phone line was silent for a moment. Campbell chewed the inside of her lip and quietly asked, "Do you think Cole is okay?"

"He's stressed, I think, and he's working a lot, but he's not out of control. He's still spending time with Tyler. In fact, he got us all courtside seats to the Pistons game last weekend. We had so much fun. He and Cole got to meet the team at halftime!"

"Seriously? Courtside seats? Meeting the team at halftime? Tyler is four years old, for crying out loud! Cole is going to ruin him! The poor kid will grow up thinking he's too good for the cheap seats! What is my brother thinking? That's not how my dad raised us."

"Listen, Campbell, I've gotta go. Tyler is stuck at the top of the playset and he wants me to help him."

"Okay. Sorry that I went bonkers on you, Jen. I'm just worried about my brother."

"I know you are. I get it."

"Tell Tyler his Aunt Cam can't wait to see him all dressed up in his tuxedo this weekend. Bye, Jen."

"I'll tell him. Goodbye, Campbell."

With so many details to pull together before the wedding, Campbell needed to get home, but her concerns about Cole drove her car thirty miles north on I-94 to Algonac, the town where Cole's lifelong best friend, Jack, lived with his wife and two young children. Throughout their lives, Jack had always kept Cole grounded. The two boys had met at summer camp in northern Michigan when they were eight years old. They looked forward to their weeks together at camp each summer, but were also dedicated to staying connected during the school year. Memories of the nights Jack had spent at the Hannigan house when they were young rolled through her mind like a film reel. Having grown up in a lower-class family, Jack was unaccustomed to the small luxuries that he enjoyed when he spent the night with Cole. Jack's family could never afford to buy the plethora of snack foods that lined the Hannigan pantry. Campbell loved watching him gorge himself on packaged oatmeal cookies, juice pouches, and, strangely, fresh fruit. She reflected on how she'd had such little awareness at the great income disparity that had existed between their families.

"I'm sorry I didn't call before just showing up like this, Jack. I didn't have your number, and I'm really worried about Cole. Today, I walked in on him snorting drugs, Jack, off of a dirty bench in a tuxedo rental dressing room. I've turned a blind eye to the variety of pills he's been taking for years, but this really scared me. Do you know anything about all of this?"

"Your brother has always partied pretty hard. I mean, all of us did when we were younger, but we all have families now. You met my kids. They watch me so close. They wanna be just like me, and that scares the hell outta me. I want them to grow up to be good people, you know? Cole invites me to go out and party like we used to, but I've just got other priorities now. And to be honest, I'm having trouble hanging with him lately. He's living pretty high on the hog, and I just can't afford the places he wants to go to. Then I feel bad when he grabs my tab at the end of the night. Last couple of years we've been drifting apart, I guess. Sure, I've seen him hit the hard stuff sometimes when we are out. I just had no idea he was doing it every day like that. I want to help, Campbell, but I'm just not sure what you think I can do for him."

Campbell sat up straight and a smile came across her face. "If you don't have plans on Saturday, you and your wife should come to my wedding! Cole would love to see you.

I think just getting back in closer touch with you might be really good for him."

"Let me talk to my wife and see if we can get a babysitter. I'd love to go to your wedding and see your family. It's been forever. And I'll do my best to talk to Cole. I'd do anything for that guy."

Campbell finished what remained of the ginger ale that Jack's welcoming wife had served her and thanked them for accommodating her unexpected visit. As she walked through their small 1950s home, toys scattered about, dirty child-sized fingerprints scattered across the walls, she felt so happy for Jack. To Campbell, it seemed that although Jack didn't have much, he had it all.

YOUR MEETING WITH LANE

Campbell hoped that Cole's friend Jack would be able to help her brother because Jack was the friend that had always kept Cole grounded. Friends like this are often not afraid to tell us the truth, but are able to communicate it with grace and love.

1. What friend in your life keeps you grounded and shares the truth with grace and love?

2. Recall a moment in your friendship where this person helped you gain some important perspective.

3. Do you have any friends outside of your financial or social class? For instance, if you are wealthy, do you have friends who are lower or middle class? What about friends of different ethnicities, careers, and educational backgrounds? How might having diversity in your friend group benefit your growth as an individual? How does having diversity in your friend group create challenges in or strain on your friendship? How can you address these challenges?

1999

A Voice from the Past

There comes to me out of the past,
A voice, whose tones are sweet and wild
Singing a song almost divine, and with a tear in every line.
—Henry Wadsworth Longfellow

"Well, aren't you a sight for sore eyes?" Debbie's unmistakable raspy voice echoed from behind Cole as she swung around and forcibly hugged the son she had been estranged from for more than a decade.

Cole didn't fight the hug in an effort to keep from causing a scene at his sister's wedding. He answered coolly, "Hello, Debbie. Doesn't Campbell look beautiful today?"

The sun shone through the church's stained-glass windows down into Tyler's young eyes. "And you must be Tyler. I am so pleased to finally meet you. I am..."

"Debbie. Tyler, this is Ms. Debbie."

Tyler squinted up into the light, reaching out his hand. "Hi, Ms. Debbie! I'm going to take some pictures, and my daddy says I have to make a nice smile. Do you think this is

141

a nice smile?" The young, blonde boy revealed both rows of teeth and gums, his face contorting into a giant, forced smile.

Tears began to form in Debbie's eyes, but she pulled herself together when she saw Cole shoot her a stern look.

"Well, yes, sir! I think that smile is just perfect, as a matter of fact! Do you think I could be in the pictures with you too?"

"As long as it's okay with my daddy. He says today is Aunt Cam's day, so we better make sure she's in the picture too."

"That's a great idea! How did you get to be so smart, young man?"

"My daddy says that I get all my smartness from my Grandpa Jim. I didn't know him because he died before I was born, but I look just like him, and I'm super smart like him too!" The boy put his hands in his pockets and swayed proudly from side to side.

Debbie kneeled down in front of Tyler, getting down to his level. Cole put his hand on his mother's shoulder, reminding her to watch her words. With a quick glance up to her son, Debbie quietly replied to her grandson.

"I knew your Grandpa Jim when he was alive, and it's true. Every word of it. You look just like him, and I'll bet that you are even smarter than he was! You probably don't even know what a lucky boy you are, do you?"

Cole reached down, putting his arm under hers, and lifted his mother back to a standing position. "Oh look, Debbie, it's Aunt Robyn. I bet it's been years since you two have had a chance to catch up."

"I'll have time to catch up with the rest of the family. It's you I've been looking forward to seeing! Look at what a handsome devil you have become, Cole. Did you bring a date to the wedding? I'd love to meet her," Debbie inquired, peering around his shoulder.

"I brought Tyler's nanny as my date."

"Oh! That must be her with Tyler. As soon as the boy ran off, she ran right over to him. She's gorgeous. You've certainly got the best of both worlds going there, don't you, dear?"

Cole ignored her digging. "Did you bring a date?"

"Oh heavens no. I've decided that men are far more trouble than they're worth. I'm enjoying the single life, spending time with my girlfriends playing bridge, and painting, and golfing, and wine club, of course."

"Sounds fascinating."

"Did you know I moved back to the area a few months ago? It's been good for me. I'm living with a friend in a lakefront home not too far from here."

"How nice for you."

"You know, Cole, now that I'm back in town, we should really get together. Go out for dinner and some drinks."

"Why would we do that?" Cole retorted.

Debbie grabbed his hand and pulled him in close, whispering so her sentiments wouldn't be overheard. "Did you ever consider that maybe I have some regrets? Maybe I'd like to apologize for all that I missed when you were growing up. I see Tyler and my heart aches to be a part of his life. Just say you're willing to give it a try for Tyler's sake."

Her words stirred a sleeping giant inside Cole. Since his childhood, he had cut Debbie out of his heart and mind like a ripped photograph, but becoming a father was changing his perspective. He desperately wished for his son to have a relationship with even one grandparent. Tyler would, of course, never have the chance to know his late grandfather, Jim. Tyler's mother, Lynne, and her parents had shown no interest in Tyler after the courts found Lynne's severe drug addiction cause to give full custody to Cole. When Lynne had realized there was no financial gain, her calls and visits to Tyler had stopped altogether. Didn't every kid need at least one grandparent in their lives? This motivation was softening his thoughts about his mother. Cole knew Debbie likely had some manipulative secondary motive, but he took the bait she had set for him. "Okay, dinner and drinks."

"The word on the street is that you really clean up at the poker table. What say we do dinner downtown, and then hit the casino? We'll make a night of it."

"The word on the street, huh?" Cole didn't trust his mother, and he harbored layers of resentment toward her, but somehow now he felt drawn to reestablishing a relationship with her.

"All right, come on. Introduce me to your girlfriend; I mean the nanny," Debbie razzed.

Downstairs in the basement of the church, one of Campbell's college friends, wearing a straight-lined periwinkle dress, searched through an overpacked canvas bag.

"I don't see it in here. What color is it?"

"It's a maroon-colored, velvety, square jewelry case. I know for sure I put it in that bag. I'm just praying Grammy Hannigan's pearls are still in there, because I never opened the box to make sure."

"Oh, you're right. It's here, and yes, the pearls are here! Something else too—looks like a note or something. Not sure what it is. I don't want to be snoopy. Here, what is this?"

Her friend looked up to see Campbell, stunning in her strapless white wedding gown with royal-blue sash that complemented her red hair with precision.

"Wow—you really look amazing!"

"Thanks! Okay, what's this about a note?"

"Here. I'm not sure what it is."

Campbell unfolded the wrinkled notebook page, which unlocked a moment she'd long forgotten. Her hand went to her mouth, and she walked over and sat down on the couch, her legs feeling wobbly.

"What is it, Campbell? Are you okay?"

Her eyes danced across the page that held her father's handwriting and a moment frozen in time.

"My dad wrote all of this down. It was years ago, when he was dying. We had this conversation…" Campbell continued reading.

Finally, after what seemed like an eternity to her friend, Campbell looked up and folded the note. "I know that this is the right thing to do."

"What is?"

"Marrying Russ. It's right this time. He's the one."

"Well, that's good, because we have to be upstairs in two minutes for pictures, and your wedding is in an hour."

Campbell laughed and rose from the chair to ensure that her eye makeup hadn't smudged during the swell of emotion. She handed the note to her friend. "Here. Read it. I had this conversation with my dad before he died. He asked me what I was looking for in a guy. I didn't even know Russ then. I had actually just started dating Britt. The characteristics I listed are nothing like Britt, but they are an exact description of Russ. See how I listed honesty? You remember the story of my first date with Russ. Tyler was a newborn, and I'd been watching him all day, and then the police showed up, and there was all this drama. Ugh—what an awful day! I didn't even have time to shower before Russ picked me up for our date. I was so distracted. I apologized for dumping all that drama on him on our first date and told him I wished I hadn't shared the events of my day with him. He got all hurt and said that if I wanted a second date with him, we both had to promise to always be honest with each other and that we would always share everything with each other, even the tough stuff, especially the tough stuff. He said honesty was the most important trait a person could have. What a coincidence that honesty is the first thing I listed here."

"Well, Russ is definitely honest. He told me I had spinach in my teeth the first night I met him. How embarrassing!"

Campbell pointed at the list from over her friend's shoulder. "I also listed compassion, family-oriented, and passionate, yet grounded."

"Russ is all of those things, especially family-oriented! I can't believe how many Wilburns traveled to Michigan for this wedding, and they are all so nice."

Campbell sat down to put on her shoes and agreed. "Yeah, he has a huge family. I can't believe they all traveled up here from Florida. Then, look, my dad added two traits at the bottom. He listed humble and devoted. I remember thinking he surprised me with what he picked."

"And those two characteristics are hard to find. Just ask your only single bridesmaid; I could tell you some stories! Truly, though, you're absolutely right, Campbell. Russ is all of these things. I'm so happy you've found such a great guy. You deserve it, my friend." The two hugged as a knock came from the old wooden church door.

Campbell opened the door and threw her arms around the woman standing stunned at the sight of the beautiful bride. "Lane! I thought you were in South Carolina for your family reunion! I'm so happy to see you! What are you doing here?"

"I guess you've not turned on the news! A hurricane has caused an evacuation of the whole area that we had booked for our reunion, so I changed our airplane tickets to Detroit. I hope you don't mind a couple of unexpected guests?"

"Are you kidding? I'm ecstatic that you're here, and I can't wait to meet your husband!"

"Well, you'll have to wait a bit longer, because they are requesting you upstairs for photos. I selfishly offered to come down to retrieve you so I could steal a moment to say hello."

"I'm so glad you did. Can you do me a favor? I can't see Russ before the wedding—bad luck, you know. Can you give him this note and tell him to read it before the wedding? It's in my dad's writing. He and I had a conversation before he died about the kind of guy I wanted to marry. My dad wrote it all down and put it in with my grandmother's pearl earrings. I guess he figured I would wear the earrings at my wedding and see the note. I forgot all about it, to be honest with you, but it's a crying shame I didn't read it before my first wedding. It would've saved me a divorce and a lot of heartache, that's for sure. Anyway, please give this to Russ and tell him I'm so excited to marry the man I've always needed in my life."

Lane took the folded note and pressed it to her chest. "I would be honored."

"You make a stunning bride, little sister," Cole admitted as he stood in his father's place in the traditional father-daughter dance at the reception.

"Thanks for filling in for Dad today, Cole."

"Of course, Cam. I'm lucky to have this dance with the prettiest girl in the room."

Campbell blushed and tears began to form in her eyes. Cole swept away the emotion that filled the space between them by changing the subject. "So you didn't tell me you invited Jack and his wife. It's really good to see them."

Campbell's stomach began to knot as she wondered if Jack had revealed to Cole how she'd tattled about his drug use. She didn't want any drama emerging on the dance floor at her wedding. "Yeah, I thought you might like to have someone to talk to besides Mom. How are things going with her?"

"Surprisingly well, actually. After I shot down her first couple of passive-aggressive digs, she chilled out. Tyler loves her, and she's been really good with him today. We actually had a really good conversation. She apologized to me, and we made dinner plans for tomorrow night."

"Wow! I'm shocked!"

"I guess maybe it's time to let bygones be bygones."

"Well I'm glad you're changing your perspective, but don't let your guard down. This is still Mom we're talking about."

"I'll keep my eyes open."

YOUR MEETING WITH LANE

Jim left Campbell an invaluable wedding gift when he placed the note from their conversation in with her grandmother's pearl earrings.

1. Looking back on the big events or moments in your own life, how did your loved ones make it special? Did you do something to remember loved ones who had passed on prior to the event?

2. Thinking of big events in the future of your own family, what can you do to make a subtle but meaningful legacy impact on the event without taking over the event?

3. What are the pros and cons of Cole getting back into a relationship with his mother, Debbie?

4. What strained relationships exist in your own family? What are the pros and cons of repairing or strengthening those relationships?

2014
Wide Sea, Small Boat

Every form of addiction is bad,
no matter whether the narcotic be alcohol, morphine, or idealism.
—Carl Jung

"Hey, Tyler, are you awake? Can I come in for a minute?" Campbell whispered through the cracked opening of the bedroom door.

A reluctant voice replied, "Sure."

She walked through the dark bedroom over to Tyler's bed where he lay under the covers. When her eyes adjusted to the darkness, she could see that his eyes were tear-stained and puffy. The clock on his nightstand read 2:04 a.m. For a moment, they sat in the silent irony of the day. Campbell wanted Tyler's graduation day to be filled with joy and celebration. Instead, it had been filled with tension and embarrassment. They both knew the situation with Cole had ruined Tyler's graduation day. What they didn't know is that Cole had just snuck back into the house after a wild night out, and was quietly listening to their conversation from outside Tyler's bedroom door. Cole could remember only hazy bits and pieces of the day, but he remembered enough to know that he had hurt the two people he loved most in the world.

Campbell broke the silence. "Tyler, I'm sorry I didn't let you go out with your friends tonight. I know it's your graduation night, and you should be out celebrating after your party, but I...I was just afraid that you would go out and do something stupid because you're angry with your dad. I couldn't let you do that. Listen, you have every right to be angry, and embarrassed, and sad. Having your dad show up at your graduation party unexpectedly like that, all drunk and obnoxious, in front of your friends, that must have been horrible. And those things he said, that you think you're better than him, that you should be kissing his ass, that you'll never get a dime of money out of him, that you're ungrateful for everything he gave you growing up...those were hurtful, toxic words. Those words came out of his addiction, his inability to process his own challenges in life. Please know that you haven't done anything wrong. He needs help, Tyler, and I'll try my best to get him motivated to find the treatment he needs. I'm just sorry I didn't get him out of there sooner. I should have had Uncle Russ take him back home right away, as soon as I saw him stumbling up the beach toward the party. I guess I just hoped that it was going to work out okay. That he would be able to just sit down, eat a hamburger and a cupcake, and celebrate your day."

"Yeah. Me too."

"He's got an addiction, Tyler. Please know that this isn't about you. Your dad's addiction to drugs and alcohol has always been his way of dealing with the stress of success. It's ironic that success brings stress, but it does. It really does. You know how your Grandpa Jim dealt with that stress?"

"How?"

"Well, he did some drinking too, and that's why I'm always on you and Jade and Jimmie about making wise choices, with addiction in the family. But, anyway, Grandpa Jim's life wasn't out of control like your dad's, and I think it's because he had another important way of dealing with his stress. He would sail the waters of the Great Lakes on his boat, and just think and process and let the waves wash it all away. One day, a couple of months before he died, he took me out on the sailboat. It was really one of the only times I remember being out there with him. Funny that it was mid-October, but we had the warmest, most beautiful day for sailing. We wore shorts and T-shirts it was so warm! We went out in the morning, and the way the sun rose, the beauty of the orange and yellow autumn leaves reflected so clearly in the water near the shore. What a beautiful day. You know, I think your dad was supposed to come with us too, but he ended up having something come up at work so he couldn't make it. Anyway, when I was out there with your Grandpa Jim, he told me that whenever he would spend the night out on the boat, he would say this prayer out loud over the open water right before he went to sleep. The prayer is called the "Breton Fisherman's Prayer, " and it goes like this:

"Dear God,
Be good to me.
The sea is so wide
And my boat is so small."

Campbell paused to let the prayer sink in and to make sure Tyler hadn't fallen asleep during her long story. When she saw that he appeared to be listening intently, she continued.

"Now, you understand that our family's wealth began with your Grandpa Jim's success. Your grandfather did not even have a college degree, but he had tenacious drive, a gifted mind, and an unstoppable work ethic. Despite all his success, he was never prideful. After sharing that prayer, he told me that the sum of his life, and all its success, was like a little boat out upon a wide sea, with wind and waves far beyond his control. He was right, because with all the money and power and prestige that he had gained, there was nothing any of us could do to help him beat his brain cancer.

"I'm telling you all of this because I want you to know, Tyler, that although our family is fortunate in many ways, life isn't anywhere near perfect. The sea is wide, and our boats are small, so we each have to find our own way to make sense of it all. I think your dad is having a lot of trouble doing that. We need each other, and we each need to find a framework to make sense of life. Anyway, I just wish I could erase today and replace it with the happy version of the day that I wished for you, Tyler, but I can't. What I can do is let you know that I love you, that I am so proud of you for your hard work in school and for handling your drunk, obnoxious father with great dignity today. I do believe you have quite a bit of your Grandpa Jim in you. I noticed it the very first moment I saw you when you were just a tiny little baby. You know, I was thinking...this summer before you start college, we should get Grandpa Jim's sailboat out of storage. Uncle Russ and I haven't taken in out since we had it repaired a few years ago! Doesn't that sound fun? Learning how to sail?"

Campbell hopped down off the bed and ruffled Tyler's hair playfully. Eavesdropping, Cole hurried back into the guest bedroom as he heard his sister starting toward Tyler's bedroom door. He eased back into the guest bed unnoticed and reflected on that prayer. Why had he never heard it from his father before? What had kept him from the sailing trip that warm October day, just weeks before his father had died?

Tyler caught his aunt's attention before she left his bedroom. "Hey, Aunt Cam?"

"Yeah?"

"I'm not mad at you for making me stay home tonight. I would've probably gotten really drunk with my friends and made an ass of myself, just like my dad. Then you'd be mad at both of us."

"Ha. True."

"I hope you don't get mad when I say this, but you don't have to try to make everything perfect all the time. Since I've been living here, and especially today, you're always trying to make everything perfect for me. I guess I appreciate you trying, but my life isn't perfect, and you can't really fix it."

"Wow, buddy. I didn't realize I was doing that." Campbell felt crushed that her efforts had added to Tyler's load of problems. "I'm sorry if I added pressure to your life by trying to make things perfect. I guess by trying so hard to help, maybe I made things harder for you. I'll try to chill out."

He continued, "But you should also know that when my dad wouldn't leave the party today and you tackled him and you both fell down rolling around in the sand? It was NOT funny at the time. It was really embarrassing actually, but that's gonna be a hilarious story one day."

"Yeah, can you believe I did that? There's always that one crazy aunt at the party, right? Please tell me no one posted pictures of that little incident on social media."

"No, I checked. Everyone was very cool about it."

"Thank goodness. Goodnight. Love you, Ty."

Campbell closed the door and quietly prayed the "Breton Fisherman's Prayer," wondering how she would handle Cole in the morning. As the end of the prayer left her lips, the image of Jack, Cole's childhood friend, flashed in her mind. She pulled her cell phone from her back pocket.

YOUR MEETING WITH LANE

Campbell tackled her intoxicated brother on the beach at Tyler's graduation party. Can you recall a high-drama situation in your family that was upsetting in the moment, but became somewhat tragically comical in hindsight?

1. Where is the problem of addiction (to substances, sex, work,) present in your life or your family members' lives? How does this addiction affect your family? What steps are you taking to provide support and treatment for the person or people struggling with addiction?

2. What healthy coping strategies do you or your family members utilize to cope with stress? Examples might include activities such as the following:
Hobbies: painting/gardening/boating/fishing/piano;
Fitness activities: running/biking/swimming/surfing
Spiritual activities: prayer/church/meditation
Emotive activities: therapy/journaling/poetry

3. The Carl Jung quote at the beginning of the chapter notes that people can be addicted to substances or to more elusive dysfunctions like idealism. In what ways is Campbell struggling with an addiction to idealism, especially with regard to her guardianship of Tyler? How can this be damaging?

2014

Wake-Up Call

A friend is one who walks in when others walk out.
—*Walter Winchell*

"Good morning, sunshine."

Cole cracked his eyes open and quickly squeezed them back shut as the morning sun pierced through the window blinds.

"Jack? What the hell are you doing here?" Cole rubbed his pounding forehead, willing his eyes to open. He reached for a bottle of pills on the nightstand.

"Your ranting sister called me last night, livid about all the excitement at Tyler's graduation party yesterday. I thought you might need a buddy, or a maybe bodyguard, to keep your sister from attacking you again, so I hopped on an airplane, and here I am. Bro, I've gotta be honest—you look like hell."

Propping himself up in the bed, Cole tried to clear the fog in his head. "Yeah, you might have to fill me in on some of the details, because I do remember keeping the flight attendant very busy pouring me drinks on the flight to Orlando yesterday and I remember driving to the beach for Tyler's party, but it gets pretty fuzzy from there." Cole threw back a handful of pills and swallowed nearly half the bottle of water Jack handed him.

"Well, let's just say that I'm recommending we get our morning coffee from the coffee shop, rather than your sister's kitchen. She may need just a bit more time to cool down before you two have your heart-to-heart talk. Come on. I came all the way to Florida. Get outta bed. We're going surfing."

By the time the two were driving to the beach with surfboards affixed to the top of the car, Cole's hangover was behind him, and he was excited to surf with his childhood best friend. He tucked away the regrets that had surfaced about the previous day's events into the basement of his mind, where he kept all the thoughts and feelings he just couldn't face.

The ocean welcomed them with a perfect day. Warm sun, tempered by a slight breeze, set the backdrop for picture-perfect waves. After several hours out on the water, they sat exhausted with their backs against the pylons of the Cocoa Beach pier, enjoying the cool shade. Cole ran his hand through his hair, pinching the tips of his light blonde curls, crusted in form by the salty water. Reaching into his cooler, he pulled out two beers, poured them into blue plastic cups, and passed one to Jack.

Despite a riptide of reluctance forming in his gut, Jack seized the quiet moment, confronting his friend. "So, you wanna talk about how your life is all blown out, or should we just keep pretending everything's cool?"

Cole took a handful of sand and threw it, side-armed, at the foamy shore. "Oh, is this why you brought me out surfing? You thought you'd bond with me first, get me feeling a little vulnerable, and then have a little post-surfing counseling session?"

Jack remained quiet, allowing Cole's defensiveness to roll out with the tide.

Cole finished his beer, poured himself another, and flipped onto his stomach, turning his face from Jack. "Do you know what it's like to lose the business your father spent his whole life building? Any idea what it feels like to see people in the community look at you with pity in their eyes? I've let my dad down. I've let the employees, the customers, and myself down. How will I ever find work again—who would hire me? Everyone in town knows about my epic screwup. It was in the newspapers, for crying out loud! And how do I make it better with Tyler when I've screwed it up so badly with him? My memory of yesterday is pretty foggy, but it seems like I crashed my own kid's grad party and made a total ass of myself. My sister hates me, and who can blame her? My dad would probably roll over in his grave if he could see what a disaster I've made of everything. It's honestly easier at this point to just let it all go. My life is officially not fixable."

With resignation, Jack looked out at the ocean, the whitecaps now disappearing as the ocean calmed. "What a waste, man." His words settled between them and then continued, "When we were kids, I thought you had it all. I'd go to your house, and you'd always have the good snacks, the cool toys and video games, and you went on these great vacations. I never had any of that. You had the family business you could take over, Cole. You were set! I just knew you had this amazing life in front of you because you had every opportunity available to you. But a few years back, I realized that none of it did you any good. The advantages you had because of your dad's business and the money, they did you more harm than good. You're rich in money, Cole, but you're poor in heart. I know having your dad die so young was really tough on you. After he died, it's like you got lost or something—you haven't been the same since then. You've never been able to commit to a girl. You've been trying to buy your way into a good relationship with Tyler, but that's not what he needs. You almost never call or want to hang out with me anymore. You're relying on drinks and drugs to get you from day to day, and it's just wrecking you, Cole. You have no purpose in life, no reason to live. You're just kind of drifting. It's like you're…empty."

Cole turned onto his back, without making eye contact, and draped his arm across his eyes, sheltering himself from the blow of his trusted friend's words. "Empty sounds about right. You know, it's like I got sick of trying to play a game I couldn't win. My dad did everything perfectly—how could I follow that? Everyone loved him. He always knew just what to do. He always closed the deal. He even somehow managed to be a decent dad in the midst of everything. I couldn't live up to any of that. And then it was like everybody was watching, just waiting for me to fail. Of course, that's just what I did, just like they all predicted. Imagine what it's like to know that you pissed away everything your dad worked so hard to build. Throughout the last decade, all I could think about is finding an escape from the pressure. So I made a lot of mistakes. Regrets piled on top of regrets, and at some point, I just threw my hands up and stopped fighting the tide of my failure. So, you say I seem empty? When I'm drunk or high, I feel empty, and trust me, it's a welcome relief."

"There's no doubt that you were always under an enormous amount of pressure, but man, aren't you sick of living like this?"

"What's the alternative?"

"Are you willing to let me help you get out of this mess?"

"Ha. I guess you can try."

"Okay, I've been thinking about this. There are four things I want you to do. First, there's a book I want you to read. It's called *The Greatest Salesman in the World*.[1] Another friend of mine who struggled with addiction read it. It really helped him. I read it on the airplane, and it's pretty good. It really changes your perspective on life."

"Read a book. I can do that."

"Second, you've got to get yourself into rehab. This outpatient counseling you did after your overdose isn't going to cut it. You are a straight-up addict. You know that, right? You're not still in denial or something like that, are you?"

"In denial? Jack, I bribe five different doctors to prescribe me drugs. Sometimes I find myself sitting in my Mercedes outside crack houses in Detroit. There's no denying I'm an addict. I'll read your book, and I'll consider rehab. What's your third request, Mr. Miyagi? Paint the fence?"

Jack nervously patted the sand in front of him, flattening it perfectly smooth. "I also want you to start coming to church with me."

"Oh, God." The hope that had been rising within Cole began to deflate. He had dug himself deeply into a hole of trouble, and the solution Jack was providing was church?

"Yes, God! Don't you ever look around and think that there must be something more than the day-to-day grind? Don't you ever think, like, who made this giant ocean?"

"I try not to think about that kind of stuff."

"You know, Cole, because of your money, you can have it all—girls, cars, houses, drugs, vacations, entertainment. You can have anything you want, but do you realize none of it's making you happy?"

"True."

"Did you hear about the research project on happiness they're doing at Harvard?[2] They're following a big group of guys, interviewing them over a lifetime, watching how they live. It's been going on for seventy-five years now. They found that there are two pillars of happiness. One is love—you've gotta open yourself up to the people closest to you, like Tyler and Campbell and me. The other pillar of happiness is finding a way to cope with the tough stuff of life in a way that doesn't push love away. I'm thinking drugs and beer are your way of coping, but that's not really working for you. I need God in my life to find purpose in this crazy world, and I need to be in church every week to keep me focused on what's important. I think if you get connected to God and find your purpose, find what you were made to do, Cole, you'll find happiness again and get yourself together."

Cole propped himself up on his elbows and initiated their first eye-contact since Jack began the conversation. "When did you become this closet God person? It's very unexpected, Jacky." He thought for a few moments, his eyes fixed on the waves, and then he continued, "What you're saying is both hopeful and seriously overwhelming. Find my purpose? Whatever. Lately, I can't even find the will to live. Listen, I will very reluctantly go to church with you—one time—but if I hate it, I'm not going back. I'm almost scared to hear your last request, but go ahead."

"I want you to move in with me for a while."

Cole laughed. "You want me to leave my penthouse bachelor pad to move into the cramped three-bedroom house you share with your wife and two kids? Why would in the world would I do that?"

"I think it'll help to have people around who care about you. It'll keep you connected and accountable. What? Is rich boy too good to live in a fifteen hundred-square-foot house on the East Side?" Jack ribbed.

"Ugh. This is getting ridiculous. Do I at least get my own room?"

"I'll move the boys into the same room together. They love to sleep together in the bunk beds anyway. It'll be great, just like being college roommates. Except for the addition of the wife and kids and the glaring lack of beer."

Cole moaned, sat up, and pushed his hand into the cooler. "Sounds like a blast, but I'm really enjoying these beach beers, so can we start all of this when we get back to Detroit? I've still got to face my sister and Tyler when we get home, so I'm not quite ready to go cold turkey just yet."

Jack poured another beer for each of them and gestured "cheers" to his friend with a wink and a smile, pleased that Cole seemed receptive to his plan.

Before Cole drank, he put his hand on his friend's shoulder. "Thanks for not giving up on me, man. You're a good friend."

"It'll be good to have you back, Cole."

YOUR MEETING WITH LANE

1. In what ways can you relate to the pressure and emptiness that Cole shares in this chapter?

2. Jack went out of his way to help his friend Cole because he had compassion for the struggles he was facing. What person came alongside you during a difficult time in your life? How might you offer gratitude for their support?

3. What person in your life right now could use your support through a difficult challenge in life? Of the five areas of capital (spiritual, social, intellectual, human, financial), which could that person benefit the most from having you invest?

4. Jack had four requests for Cole:
   - Move in with Jack and his family
   - Go to church with Jack and his family
   - Go to rehab and get sober
   - Read *The Greatest Salesman in the World* by Og Mandino

   What do you think motivated Jack's choice of each one of the items on this list? Why did he think these were the most important changes for Cole to make?

1993

The Butterfly Trust

To become a butterfly, metamorphosis is necessary.
If the caterpillar never went through this process of change,
it would never achieve its great destiny
and become its most glorious self.
—Michelle "Chaella" Boddie

Campbell nervously wiped a wet rag across the clean kitchen counter for the third time that morning. "Dad, are you sure you have the strength to do this?"

"I've been looking forward to this meeting for weeks. This may be the last time I'm able to offer my insights to the advisor team. I'll be fine. We'll need to bring the walker, though. I'm not feeling very steady on my feet today."

"I already have it in the trunk of the car. I still say we should've had everyone come here to the house for the meeting. It takes so much out of you when you leave home."

Jim waved his hand dismissively. "I'm so tired of looking at these walls. I need to get out of this house every so often to remember that there's still a whole world out there."

Despite the brave front she displayed to her father, Campbell battled a dozen butterflies swarming in her stomach. Her dad was right. This meeting would likely be the last one her father would have with his advisors, and it would require her to digest heavy loads of legal and financial information, a task made no less difficult by her recent lack of sleep, as her caregiving role had become more challenging.

After the struggle of patience and physical strength required to get Jim to the lawyer's office, Campbell peeked around the door to the conference room that held a mahogany table large enough to accommodate Jim, Cynthia, Lane, Cole, Campbell, two financial advisors, two attorneys, and an accountant. Jim had insisted on arriving early to avoid making a display of himself struggling to walk into the room. The cancer had moved to his bones, his right hip and lower spine most affected, which caused significant trouble with movement in his right leg. Campbell got him settled in his chair, poured him a glass of water to relieve the dry mouth he endured as a side effect of the radiation, and tucked his walker off into the corner before the others arrived.

Campbell snuck out to use the bathroom down the hall before the meeting began. As she turned the corner, she was greeted by a wall of people in suits.

"Oh, Campbell, look at you! I haven't seen you since you were this tall!" A woman held her hand in the air waist high, and peered at her with doting typically reserved for newborn babies.

One of the suited men also chimed in, "Do you remember me?"

"Um. I'm afraid I don't. I'm sorry," Campbell replied.

He held out his hand. "Mr. Jefferson. Your father's

accountant. He and I have worked together for years. I'm sorry to hear what you're going through with your dad, being so young and all."

Campbell shuffled nervously, managing a full bladder and her fears that the advisor team still viewed her as a child. "Yes, your name sounds familiar now. I'm sorry. Listen, I need to use the restroom before we begin. My dad is in the conference room, so feel free to head on in."

"Great to see you, Jim. Glad you could make it." With each handshake from Jim's team of advisors, he saw in their eyes a subtle sadness at the sight of him, pallid and thin. Even Cole, the last of the meeting's attendees to enter the conference room, looked shocked at the ironic and harsh sight of his father, looking frail in his power position at the head of the conference table, bald and drowning in his now-oversized blue blazer.

The team passed out a stack of booklets to each person. The lawyers began, sharing the overview of Jim's estate, mostly for the benefit of Campbell and Cole, who had not yet been given full disclosure of the compendium of legal and financial instruments their father's estate contained. They spoke of life insurance policies, irrevocable and revocable trusts, promissory notes between one business and the other. Campbell had no idea that the company she knew as Hannigan Industries was actually comprised of three separate businesses, one holding the land and building, one holding the machinery, and one holding the service and parts aspect of the business. For a fleeting moment, she almost admitted to herself that her father may have been right in wishing she had taken some business classes. But what class could have prepared her for this? Even Cole, who was already well aware of many details regarding the business, looked glassy-eyed and overwhelmed by the complexity of the information being shared.

"I know this is a lot to take in, so if you'll turn to page four of your booklet, you'll see a one-page abridgment. Cole and Campbell, your pages are each customized to reflect the details unique to your individual portfolios. Typically, we have these meetings postmortem, but your father wanted to ensure that you have a full understanding of the way he has divided his assets between you. Cole, you'll see that you will retain the business and the machinery aspects of the company, while Campbell, you'll retain the Hannigan Industries land holdings as well as a greater portion of your father's personal investment capital to account for the value of the business going to Cole. Essentially, Hannigan Industries, owned by Cole, will pay rent to Hannigan Land Holdings, held by Campbell, for use of the land and building. Cole and Jim both shook their heads in agreement, as if this had been something they'd decided long ago.

Campbell's throat tightened. "I think that...I think that feels a little strange to me." Nine pairs of eyes stared blankly back at her. "I mean, let's just simplify the plan and give the whole business to Cole, all three parts or whatever."

The pairs of eyes now began glancing around at each other, and Campbell suddenly felt like a child sitting erroneously at the adult table for Thanksgiving dinner. Jim chimed in, "Well, honey, my reasoning behind that decision was that this way, you'll always have your own income."

Campbell fiddled her pen nervously in her hands. "With all due respect, Dad, it won't really be my income anyway; I'm not doing anything for it. It will probably just complicate things for Cole. Is there a problem that I'm not foreseeing with giving Cole all three business entities, and giving me a greater portion of the money?"

All eyes turned to Jim, who thought briefly and then joked as if Campbell wasn't present. "Now do you all understand why I always say that it's Campbell who is responsible for all these gray hairs?" He rubbed his head, suddenly remembering his gray hair was now gone due to the radiation treatments. "Cole, how do you feel about what Campbell is proposing?"

"Fine by me," Cole replied.

With reluctance in his voice, Jim directed, "Okay, let's change the plan as Campbell has proposed." Then, speaking directly to the investment team, he continued, "Now listen, I know she's young, but I don't want her in some overly-aggressive investment strategy. You make sure she's diversified to protect her assets no matter what happens, because without those land holdings, she won't have much backup if the market crashes."

"Yes, sir," they all replied in staggered unison, and a woman from the investment management firm wrote feverishly in her booklet.

When the investment portion of the meeting began, Campbell tried to sharpen her focus, taking a long sip of her coffee and readying herself to take copious notes. Whenever the professionals used trade language that Jim suspected Campbell or Cole wouldn't understand, he either offered a brief explanation himself or encouraged the advisors to do so. Finally, after three such interruptions, Jim made an attempt to change the tone of the meeting.

"Excuse me for interrupting again, but one of my goals for this meeting is to make sure that everyone understands my expectations about how things will run in my absence. Listen, kids, you have a responsibility to stay informed about how your money is being handled. If that means you have to interrupt these folks when they are speaking, to ask a question or even to offer a different perspective, that's what I expect you to do. Now to the advisor team, we all understand that with money comes power. You would surely never hand someone a weapon without teaching them how to use it, would you? I believe you people have an ethical responsibility to keep your young clients here informed. Campbell, especially, hasn't been exposed to any of this kind of information before, and I'm sure you can understand how overwhelming it must be. We've all been working together for years complicating this estate, and it makes good sense to all of us, but my kids are seeing most of it for the first time. Now I understand that it will take some extra time for you to slow down to explain and re-explain the accounts, the estate plan, and all of the associated trade language, but that's what I'm asking you to do, both now and after I'm no longer attending these meetings with all of you."

The client relationship manager, who had stopped writing notes with her pen, spoke up, "I understand. I'll make a note in all of your accounts to ensure that we take this approach at all future meetings, Mr. Hannigan. I'm sorry we didn't anticipate your needs today, but I'm certain that Frank can accommodate your request with the remainder of his presentation." She looked over the top of her reading glasses at her colleague.

"Yes, certainly." Frank shifted in his chair.

"Thank you," Jim and Campbell replied in unison while Cole nodded in agreement.

Lane jumped in, her British accent standing out. "I'd be pleased to refer you to my colleagues who hold training events for advisors on the topic of taking a legacy approach with the next generation of their client families. You may know that the harsh reality is less than twenty percent of inheritors retain their parent's advisors.[1] Turns out, it's a lack of relationship with the advisors that's the number—one reason cited for breaking the relationship, which is a fact that properly makes the case for an overt multigenerational approach. I'll forward that information to you after the meeting." Lane smiled and nodded in the direction of the client relationship manager.

"Yes, please do. We'd love to add something like that to our continuing education schedule." The client relationship manager dutifully concurred and picked up her pen to make a note of it.

"Forgive my boldness, but I'd like to propose adjusting our course for the remainder of the meeting." As Lane continued, Frank sat back and rocked in his chair, red-faced and working hard to maintain his patience. "I fear Jim's energy may be waning, and we need him at his best for the legacy portion of this meeting, which is absolutely vital to the health of the Hannigan family. Jim, are you comfortable with terminating further discussion of the estate plan and financial accounts at this time and moving onto discussion of your ethical will so that we can provide Campbell and Cole, as well as the advisors on the team, a framework with which to approach the future handling of your estate?" Looking for permission, Lane glanced over at Jim.

"I think that sounds like a good idea, Lane. Let's proceed with that, then." Jim ran his finger nervously back and forth across the top of his paperwork. Cole glanced at Frank and rolled his eyes subtly enough that their communication stayed hidden from all the others at the table. The two had built camaraderie at the bar after several previous advisor meetings Cole had attended with his father. Neither was excited about the touchy-feely direction Lane was leading. With so many important decisions to make, there was no time to waste.

Lane handed out a page to each person at the table. "Up until this point, we've been discussing how to prepare Jim's assets for the family. What I'd like to focus on now is how to prepare the family for the assets. This page reflects a snapshot of the work he and I have been doing together in the last several weeks. Take it away, Jim!"

Jim put on his reading glasses and began. "Okay, well, you can see on the page in front of you that for each of the three areas I'll be addressing, Lane asked me to choose a symbol. For the first section, titled *Our Family Legacy*, the symbol I chose is an assembly line. Some of you know that my grandfather immigrated to America from Ireland. Because he struggled to get work as an immigrant, he was stuck doing some pretty brutal factory work. My father followed after him in the same line of work. Both of them worked very hard at extremely difficult work to provide even the most basic needs for their families, and I respect them for it. I saw the toll their work took on them, and I wanted something more for my life, and for you kids, so I took the work ethic they passed down to me and used it to move up the ladder in the automotive industry. See, I believe that failure only exists for those who quit trying. So I kept trying until I reached my goal, and then I set new goals and reached for those. An assembly line just keeps producing, and producing, and producing. Always producing something of value to the world. My father and grandfather worked their fingers to the bone on that assembly line, and I have nothing but gratitude and respect for them. Me? I am the assembly line." Jim tapped his finger against his chest and then pointed it toward Campbell and Cole. "We aren't put here on this earth just to suck air; we're here to make something of ourselves, to produce something of value through hard work. That's what I expect from both of you."

The room grew quiet, and the tension that had been building in the room after Lane's interruption evaporated in the presence of Jim's heartfelt words.

"The next section is titled *Behind the Scenes Values*, and allows me to share some things you probably didn't know about me, areas of myself I didn't always share. I thought a boat would symbolize this section best. You both know I love my sailboat, but the part you probably don't know, and I don't know why I never shared it with you, is that I enjoyed being out on the water because it made me feel small. I know that I always act like the big cheese, as if I have everything under control, but the truth is, I've always looked to God for direction and to keep me grounded. That perspective kept me focused on the right values— family, honesty, humility. I showed you my work ethic, but I'm not sure I showed you my softer side. My motivation behind trying to work hard and succeed was to give you both a good life, because I want the best for you; I love you both very much. Now I want you to work hard in life, but I also hope you each find your own way of making peace with God like I did out on the sailboat. That's all I'll say for that."

Campbell pulled a tissue out of her pocket and dabbed at the corner of her eyes while Cole pinched his nose in between his eyes, pushing tears back. The team of advisors, voyeurs to this sacred family moment, all sat in perfect silence.

"And the final section is titled *The Meaning of the Money*. The symbol I picked here is a butterfly. As we all know, a butterfly starts out as a caterpillar. The process of transformation it undergoes while in its chrysalis, and the struggle the newly-formed butterfly takes as it breaks out of it, are vital to its life and function as a butterfly. I'm your dad, so even though you're both adults, well, I still see you as caterpillars. There's no doubt that my death, and your subsequent inheritance, will bring about a struggle of grief and identity. This money will provide a chrysalis for you, containing resources that have the potential to help transform your life into something even more beautiful. You might be tempted to simply bask in this wealth, remaining inside the chrysalis, but if you do, you'll never become the people you were created to be, and it will ultimately consume you. I expect that the money you receive will be utilized to strengthen you to fly boldly in the direction of your goals. I want it used for education, freedom of choice, pursuit of career goals, charitable giving, family connection, and generosity. It is absolutely vital that you pass down these values to your children, so the impact of my legacy remains for their children and beyond. To serve as a reminder of these ideals, I am changing the name of the largest trust, from which most of your distributions will come across your lifetime, to The Butterfly Trust."

YOUR MEETING WITH LANE

1. During the financial meeting, Campbell learned of an estate-planning decision Jim had made that didn't sit well with her. She didn't like the idea of getting monthly lease income from the business. What do you suppose felt uncomfortable to Campbell about this plan?

2. It is not uncommon for wealth creators to have an authoritative style in estate planning and family management. After all, it's their money, right? What are the benefits of remaining open to the voice of rising generations? What are the risks?

3. How can wealth creators maintain decision-making power while still remaining open to the voice and experience of rising generations?

4. If you could give some advice to the legal and financial advisors prior to the meeting, what might you say? What did they do well during the meeting? What might they have handled better?

5. Discuss the significance of Jim naming his trust "The Butterfly Trust." How might naming the trust impact his family and/or advisors in the future?

(continued)

6. Complete the exercise Jim shared with his family at the meeting.

   Our Family Legacy - What symbol represents your family legacy?

   Behind the Scenes Values - What one thing should your family members know about the internal values that drive your approach to wealth and your approach to life in general? Focus on the values you have perhaps hidden or been less overt in sharing.

   The Meaning of Money - Define a specific vision for what you hope the impact of your financial legacy will be.

2008

Hard Times

Wealth, my son, should never be your goal in life.
True wealth is of the heart, not of the purse.
—Og Mandino, The Greatest Salesman in the World

Campbell nervously ran her index finger around the rim of her wine glass, staring deeply into its dark red depth. Russ looked over first at his mother-in-law, Debbie, then at his seven-year-old twins, and then at his wife.

"Debbie, it's good to see you. What has it been, about two years?" Russ inquired casually.

"It has! I can't believe how big Jade and Jimmie have gotten. I hate that you live so far away. I feel like I miss out on seeing them grow up," Debbie whined.

"Well, Mom, you know you're welcome to visit anytime." Campbell dodged the blow of her mother's manipulation.

"Actually, that's something I wanted to talk with you both about."

Campbell shot Russ a nervous glance, uncertain where her mother was going with this dinner conversation taking place in front of her children.

"Well, you know I've been living with Cole since I moved back to Detroit. That worked out well for several years. I was there to help out with Tyler and everything. But Cole's going through a tough time, and we're realizing that our arrangement isn't working out very well anymore."

"What do you mean?" Worry mounted in Campbell's voice.

"Well, he's been under a lot of stress at work. I don't think the business has been doing very well. He's been just awful to me, snapping at me, and this weekend, he asked me to move out. I know what his problem is. I guess Tyler's getting old enough that he doesn't need me around as much, so he's kicking me out on my keister."

Without thinking, Campbell shared too much. "That's interesting, because Cynthia, Dad's old assistant, called me last week. I guess Cole hired a new assistant and moved Cynthia into human resources, doing health insurance and payroll. Anyway, she told me that this recession is really hitting them hard. Cole expanded so quickly around the time we got married; now with this bad economy, they haven't been able to recover."

"Uncle Cole?" Young Jade inquired. "I wish he was here. I love it when he does that funny trick where he pulls the end of his thumb off!"

Realizing the kids were picking up on the negative tone of their conversation, Russ followed Jade's lead.

"You're right, Jade. That trick is funny, isn't it? I almost called 911 last time he did it because I thought for sure he'd need stitches to reattach the end of his thumb. Although,

I have to tell you, that trick has nothing on the trick where your daddy pulls a quarter out of your ear, right, baby?" Russ wanted to protect his children from becoming concerned about their uncle, but he was equally curious about the direction Debbie seemed to be moving the conversation.

As expected, Debbie continued, "This recession has hit us all hard. I shudder to tell you how much money I've lost in the market. I lost just about everything I had. Everyone knows I didn't get anywhere near the settlement I could have gotten when your father and I divorced, so I don't have the luxury of a safety net like you and your brother. And I'm afraid my credit is less than perfect after my lousy ex-husband foreclosed on our apartment in Chicago. So since your brother is kicking me out, I've got nowhere to go."

"What are you going to do, Mom?" Campbell's stomach tightened.

"This recession is really bad, Campbell. I'm out of options. I hoped you'd be willing to take me for a while."

The kids erupted with excitement. "Yay, Grandma's gonna stay!"

Campbell raised her finger to her children. "The grown-ups need to discuss this. Mom, I'm very sorry about what's happened with Cole, and I'm sorry the recession has hit you so hard, but let's continue this discussion later tonight."

"Okay, okay," Debbie agreed.

In his most studious voice, Jimmie made an attempt to participate in the conversation. "My social studies teacher taught us about the global recession. I know all about what you guys are talking about."

"What in the world, child? Are you seven or twenty-seven years old? I know you did not get that brain capacity from my side of the family." Russ squeezed the plastic rim from the milk jug cap between his thumb and index finger until it flicked across the table, hitting Jimmie in the chest. A vociferous burst of giggles poured out from both children, bursting the tension hovering in the room.

When their laughter had subsided, Campbell followed up with the kids. "So, you're right, we are in a global recession, which means that money can be harder to come by for both businesses and for families. It makes everything a little more complicated, but I don't want you guys to worry about it. Do you know why?"

"Why?" both kids replied in unison.

"Well, because our family has plenty of money to pay our bills, and even some money for some extra stuff. But money isn't the most important thing anyway. Family and faith are our most valuable treasures. We are rich in love."

"Yes, we are." Russ patted his wife's leg under the table, proud of the direction she was taking the uncomfortable conversation.

"Oh, we talked about treasure at Sunday school this week," Jade added. "We put on these funny pirate eye patches and marched around saying, 'Where your treasure is, there your heart will be, mateys!'"

"That was fun," Jimmie giggled.

Picking the chicken out of his teeth with a toothpick, Russ asked, "What do ya'll think that means?" Both kids stared blankly back at their parents.

Campbell took her napkin off her lap and placed it on the table. "Bible verses make more sense if you read the whole section rather than just the one sentence. That way you can get the full meaning." Campbell grabbed the family

Bible off the shelf and read a few verses. "'Do not store up for yourselves treasures on earth, where moths and vermin destroy, and where thieves break in and steal. But store up for yourselves treasures in heaven…For where your treasure is, there your heart will be also.'"[1]

Jimmie thought for a moment, raised his hand and began, "I know what it means. It means that if you love the forever kind of stuff like God, and your family, and your friends, and helping others, nobody can take that away from you, so you'll always be okay. But if you love your big house, or your cool toys, or your allowance the most, somebody could take those things, or they might break or get ruined because you left your stuff out in the rain, or you might lose them because of a recession, and then you would feel like you lost everything that was important to you, when really none of that is the important stuff."

Campbell winked at her son. "That's right, little man. So no matter what happens, a recession or whatever, we will always be okay as long as we make God and each other the most important things, our treasures."

Debbie jumped in, disgusted by the seemingly perfect family moment, "Well that's easy to say, but when you're worried where you'll lay your head at night, the money stays at the forefront of your mind."

Russ transitioned, "I'm thinking it's time for our little treasures to do some dishes!"

"Noooo!" the twins replied.

"No complaints or I'll make you clean Mommy's dirty oven, and trust me, you do NOT want that punishment." Russ watched the kids clear the dishes into the kitchen, and then quietly addressed Debbie. "Debbie, your daughter and

I are trying to be intentional about what we share with the kids at their young age, so we expect that from now on you will keep conversations about money and family problems between the adults."

Debbie smiled coolly. "Of course." Then she continued, "You know, I see how busy the two of you are. Campbell, you were too late getting home from teaching at the college to get the kids off the bus. Russ, it sounds like the Walker house you're building was supposed to be completed weeks ago, and now that new condominium build starts next week? I could really take some pressure off the two of you around here by helping out with the house and the kids. Why don't you let me move in and help you out?"

Campbell took a long sip of her wine and passed it to her husband, who did the same. "Let's talk about this later tonight, Mom."

After dinner, Russ and Campbell took a walk while the kids stayed back at home with Debbie. "You're right, Russ. We're overwhelmed and definitely need some extra help around the house, but having my mom live with us is not the only answer. Maybe getting a babysitter to help us out a few afternoons a week is the best idea."

"Of course it's the best idea. It's my idea." Russ playfully grabbed his wife's hand as they walked. "So, what are we going to do about your mom having no place to live?"

"That part is trickier. I just can't believe she's blown through all the money she got in the divorce settlement! Do you think that's really true?"

"Well, I guess there's only one way to know. If she's really in financial trouble and needs help, ask her for total transparency. Tell her to show you her financial statements, and you can help her sort her income and expenses and put together a budget. No sense in helping her out if she's got no plan to improve her financial situation, right?"

"That seems really logical. Do you think she'll agree to be that transparent?"

"Well, if she's really out of money, I guess she won't have a choice. And if she's not willing to be honest with you about it, well then maybe that's a sign that she can find a way to handle her own hard times. If you could ask your dad about this, what do you think he would tell you to do?"

Campbell walked and thought for a few moments. "You know, I was so young when my dad died, sometimes I don't know if I'm remembering him as he was or if I'm filling in the gaps on my own. Does that make sense?"

"Sure."

"Sometimes I wish he had written down more of his wishes explicitly, so I could go back and reference how he wanted me to use the money. He knew I'd have trouble with my mom—we talked about that. He was just as annoyed by her manipulation as the rest of us, but I know he still cared about her. I just wish my dad and I had talked about whether he would have wanted me to support her financially when she finally ran out of money."

"I wish we could ask him about that too. That would make this decision a whole lot easier. But since we don't have that opportunity, we're just going to have to trust our best judgment. You've got that Hannigan blood running through your veins, and I think you have great instincts, so maybe you should trust yourself a little more."

After the kids were asleep, Campbell and Russ readdressed the difficult topic with Debbie.

"Please keep your voice down, Mom. The kids are sleeping."

"I just can't believe what you're asking of me. You're treating me like a child! You may have more money than me, darling, but lest you forget, I am still your mother!"

"Mom, we are just trying to help you get..."

"I am fully capable of keeping a budget and maintaining my own checkbook, thank you very much. I've been doing it longer than you've been alive! You're just like Cole. You both treat me like I'm some kind of—"

"Mom, please, no one is saying you aren't capable. And speaking of Cole, what on earth happened between you two? What did you do that made him kick you out?"

"Well, I made the mistake of getting into a conversation with Cole about your father."

"Okay, and that didn't go well, I take it?"

"No, it didn't go well, obviously." Debbie lit a cigarette, despite the fact that Russ and Campbell had asked her to smoke outside. Campbell looked at Russ, who returned a glance indicating she should let it go this time.

"So what happened?"

"I don't know. He got all offended. I must have hit a hot button or something. He's so easy to offend these days—always all hopped up on some drug or another."

"Mom, what did you say about Dad?"

"Well, I told Cole he should have never taken over the business."

"Why?"

"I said that damn business was ruining him, just like it ruined your father."

186

"Well, no surprise that comment wasn't received well." Campbell sat back in her chair.

"He started whining about how he had no choice in taking over the business. I told him that was a cop-out. He said he felt all this pressure from your dad to take over, and that I didn't understand what it was like to be sucked into the black hole of Jim Hannigan's legacy.[2] I told him to stop his whining. He could have chosen another career path. Now, I'll be the first to tell you that your father was way over the top in preaching a strong work ethic to you and your brother. I got so sick of hearing him shove that down your throats as you kids were growing up. 'How about teaching the kids to enjoy their lives a little?' I would say to him. But I'll tell you, I know your father and he would have never made Cole believe he had no choice in taking over the business. I told him that if he doesn't get over this issue, he'll find himself sitting there one day holding a gun to his own head from all the pressure. That's when he told me to pack my things and get out."

"Oh, for heaven's sake, Mom, that image seems a little dramatic, don't you think? No wonder he reacted so strongly."

"I deal in drama, Cammie, you know that." She exhaled a puff of smoke from her lungs and put out her cigarette on the plate that held crumbs of the cheesecake she had eaten for dessert. "But I wasn't being dramatic when I said that. I'm worried about your brother, Campbell. He's putting a lot of pressure on his own shoulders. Your father's legacy looms over his shoulder in ways larger than Jim ever intended, and Cole's gonna crack, you mark my words. Either that or he's going to lose the business."

"Lose the business?"

"I've been hearing around town he's got that business way underwater. One night a couple weeks ago, he came home drunk or high, ranting that if things didn't get better, he'd be sitting at an auction watching his father's legacy get ripped from his hands. Those are his words, not mine. I'm telling you, that boy is under a lot of pressure, and he's heading down a path of destruction, one way or another."

"It's almost like you'll be pleased to see it happen," Campbell said in disgust.

Debbie snapped back, "A mother never wants to see her children suffer, but when Cole falls apart, you all just remember that you heard it here first."

The normally patient Russ rolled his eyes at the way Debbie spoke so casually about her own son's demise. It was time to set some boundaries and get the conversation back on track. "Let's get back to this issue of your financial situation and where you're going to live, Debbie."

Campbell took her husband's lead. "We appreciate your offer to help out with the kids, Mom, but having you live here is not going to work out. Russ and I talked after dinner, and then I called Cole to talk to him about this. We all agree that you should go back to Michigan where your friends are, and live on your own. Cole and I are willing to help you buy a decent condo, but you're going to have to get a job to pay for your own expenses."

"A decent condo?" Debbie lit another cigarette. "How generous of you," she said sarcastically, taking a long drag. "I don't want you kids to worry your little hearts about me. I'll be on a plane tomorrow. I understand that you don't want me in your happy little world down here in Florida, but I'll take whatever help you're offering. Thank you for helping me get into a decent condo. I guess you and your brother will never understand that when you fall on hard times, you'll take any help you can get." Debbie stood, leaving her plate on the table, went into the guest bedroom, and closed the door.

YOUR MEETING WITH LANE

1. How much fear do you live with on a daily basis about losing your financial security (the value of your assets) as a result of a recession or stock market crash?

2. Campbell's family discussion of a Bible verse at the dinner table invested spiritual capital into their family and taught important values. Think about a hot topic that's been on the minds of your family or the culture at large. What's one thing you can do this week to leverage that open door to have an important values-based conversation with your loved ones?

3. Campbell took a unique approach during the family's discussion about treasure. Instead of telling everyone what she thought the Bible verse meant, she found a way to unlock the kids' thoughts about it. In a sense, she allowed her son, Jimmie, to turn on the lightbulb in his own mind, which allowed him to have more ownership of the values he shared. Consider the last conversation you had with someone in the generation below you. How might it have gone differently if you had asked more questions and held your own convictions back until the end, or perhaps not shared them at all?

4. Campbell and Russ struggle to decide the right approach in helping Debbie deal with her hard times. What is the right approach in helping family/friends who seek your financial support?

Early 2001

Life at Auction

*It is very hard to stay in touch with our true identity
because those who want our money, our time, and our energy
profit more from our insecurity and fears
than from our inner freedom.*
—*Henri M. Nouwen*

As Cole emerged from sleep into consciousness, an old, familiar sense of dread filled his stomach. He had done his best to keep himself numbed from his brutal current reality, but there was always that pesky moment where he woke up to realize he was still stuck in his hopeless life. What would his father say if he could see how Cole had wasted all the opportunity he had given him? The previous day had brought with it news of the moment he'd feared since the day his father had died almost eighteen years ago. Cole had lost Hannigan Industries. The company his father had built was going to auction. It had become clear over the past several months that there was no way for him to recover the business. He had expanded too fast. The economic downturn had hit him too hard, and he just couldn't turn the business around. His dad used to say, "Failure only exists for those who quit trying." He felt like he had tried as hard as he could, working twelve-hour days, seven days a week, and he was still losing the business. Of course, he had made some risky moves to expand the business, but he had felt that this was the only way to keep the business growing. He had also been living pretty hard outside of work, and the impact of living life hard and fast was catching up with him as he got older.

Cole turned over in the bed and gazed upon the beautiful brunette lying next to him. She roused at the sound of his movement.

"Good morning." She put her hand over her eyes to block the light. "Ouch. Does your head hurt as bad as mine does?"

Cole reached over to the nightstand to grab a bottle of pills, and offered one to her.

"What am I taking?"

"Do you want your headache to go away? Just take it. You weren't very worried last night about what I was giving you."

She giggled, swallowed the pill with some water, and settled back on the pillow, intertwining her legs around his under the covers.

Cole let the comfort of her closeness sink in. He wasn't in love with her, but she was his favorite. In that moment, he needed to know what motivated her to say yes to him all the nights he had invited her to party or spend the night. "Let me ask you something. If I was a nobody—if I lost Hannigan Industries somehow and was just some guy you met at a bar—would you want anything to do with me? Would you be lying in my bed right now?"

Seemingly surprised by the question, she let a small giggle slip out, and then replied, "I can't imagine who you would be if you weren't Cole from Hannigan. You are Hannigan Industries, baby, so why the hell are you asking crazy questions so early in the morning?" She gave his legs a squeeze between hers.

Deflecting, Cole slid out of the bed. "I think I just need some coffee. You want some?"

"Desperately."

As he walked to the kitchen, anxiety welled up in Cole's chest. He swallowed a Xanax to quell it. The pill swirled around in his empty stomach along with the painkiller had already taken upon waking. He thought of the week ahead. The auction was Friday. This time next week, someone else, some vulture, would be the owner of the business his father had built. How had he allowed his life to get so out of control? Underneath the disappointment and embarrassment of losing the business was something more ominous. He agreed with the beautiful girl in his bed: he was nothing if he wasn't the owner of Hannigan Industries.

He needed to call Campbell to tell her. What would he say to her? What would she think? She had never wanted the business, but she would surely be devastated to learn that her brother had driven it into the ground. The thought of hearing the disappointment in her voice was more than he could bear, so he took out his phone to text her the bad news. It made his stomach sink just to see the words on the screen. He pushed the button that sent the message, and it all suddenly felt real. He set his phone down on the counter and began making coffee. Within a minute of sending the text message, his phone began to ring. Looking down to see his sister's name and picture on the screen, he pressed the button to ignore the call and focused on the coffee dripping into the pot. He pushed down the anger, the fear, and the shame. All at once, an idea struck him. He climbed the stairs to the bedroom with two cups of coffee in hand.

"I feel like doing something crazy, getting the hell out of town. I've always wanted to go to Prague. Do you want to go to Prague with me? It's still early—I'm sure we can get a flight today. I've got to be back home by Thursday night, but that will give us plenty of time. Come on, get up, you've got to go home and pack. Just make sure you bring that red dress I bought you. You know I love that red dress." He stretched across the bed and kissed her.

She pulled away and leaned her head back as a smile spread across her face. "You're crazy, you know that? How could I say no Prague with Cole Hannigan? Of course I'll go with you."

MEETING WITH LANE

1. In this chapter, we learn that Cole is losing the family business. Looking back over the past eighteen years since Jim died, what factors led to the demise of the business?

2. What concerns do you have about Cole now?

3. What motivated his impulsive decision to go to Prague?

4. If you could go back to the time that Cole took over the business when his father was dying, what advice would you give him personally? Describe what business succession plan might have helped avoid this outcome. What conversations should Jim and Cole have had prior to Jim's death?

5. Apply this situation to your own life. How might you take the advice you would have given Cole to improve your own family business or individual leadership in your own family?

Late 2011

Plan B

One day you will do things for me that you hate.
That is what it means to be family.
—*Jonathan Safran Foer,* Everything Is Illuminated

It was still dark outside as Campbell walked across the cold tile floors on her way to the coffeepot. Her morning coffee was something she looked forward to each night as she settled into bed. Her cellphone rang, and she looked at the screen to see who could be calling her before 6 a.m.

"Tyler?"

"Aunt Campbell?"

"Is everything okay? What's going on?"

"I wasn't sure who to call. My dad won't wake up. I got up for school a few minutes ago and found him on the couch. He's breathing, but only really small breaths. And I can't wake him up no matter what I do.

"Is Bianca there?"

"Bianca? No, dad fired her a few months ago, and he didn't get another nanny. I mean, I'm gonna be sixteen in a few months, so it's not really necessary."

"Okay. Try to wake him up again. Pat the side of his face. Be loud. Lift up his arm and let it fall down. Shake his shoulders."

Tyler went about following her instructions to rouse his father, but he had no success. Campbell heard the concern in Tyler's voice rising.

"Okay, Tyler, I know this is scary, but I need you to go get the house phone and call 911."

"911?"

"Call 911."

"Is he gonna die?"

"Tyler, don't hang up your cell phone. Just go get the house phone and call 911. I'll be in your other ear telling you what to say to them when they answer.

"Okay. Okay. I'm going to get the phone."

In the meantime, Campbell rushed into her bedroom where Russ was sleeping with the family's dachshund curled up at his chest.

"Russ—wake up. My brother's in trouble. I've got to get to Michigan right away."

"I'm up. I'm up. What's going on?" Russ lifted his head off the pillow, confused and sleepy-eyed.

"I've got Tyler on the phone right now. He's calling 911. Cole's unconscious. I've got to get there right away."

"Okay. You get yourself ready. I'll hop online and get you a flight."

Campbell only half-listened to her husband, her attention fixed on the words Tyler shared with the emergency operator.

"You're doing great, buddy. Tell them his breathing is very shallow."

Pain rose in Campbell's heart as she heard Tyler continue, "Yeah, he was in really bad shape last night. He was really mad and throwing things around and yelling. No, I'm not sure what drugs he took, but I see cocaine and pill bottles around the house sometimes. I know he was drinking whiskey. Um, I went to bed around 11 p.m. No, I didn't see him after that. I shouldn't have left him alone. I don't know why I didn't check on him. Okay, I know. Are they almost here?"

When she heard a break in Tyler's conversation with the dispatcher, Campbell jumped in to comfort him. "Tyler, can you hear me? I'm coming to you now. I'm going to be there as fast as I can, buddy. You are not doing this alone. I am right here with you."

In a whirlwind, Campbell made her way to the airport, her stomach sick with worry. She found her assigned seat on the plane and got settled, realizing quickly that all the planning and rushing to get out of town had provided a welcomed distraction. Now, looking out the airplane window, she had nothing to distract her from her worries. This feeling was all too familiar. She remembered a similar flight from Orlando to Detroit to meet her father at the hospital. Now it was her brother. She knew Cole had been reeling since losing the business earlier in the year, but she had no idea how bad things had gotten. He'd been avoiding conversation with her as much as possible, ignoring her calls and acting distant whenever they talked. Now all she could hope for was another opportunity to talk with him. She looked back with regret on that first conversation they'd had after the business had been sold at auction. There were harsh things she wanted to say out of anger in that moment, but she held back, not wanting to make things worse for him. What she really regretted was all that she didn't say—the words he probably most needed to hear from her. She never said she forgave him. She never told him that having him alive and well had far more value to her than the family business. Those sentiments were all true, but she hadn't shared them, and now maybe she had lost her chance.

"Traveling for business or pleasure?" The man sitting in the aisle seat leaned across the empty middle seat between them and made an attempt to start a conversation. Campbell noticed he wasn't wearing a wedding ring and worried about his intentions. She didn't feel up to having small talk anyway.

"Um. Business," she lied with a contrived smile, and then returned her focus to the puffy white clouds outside the airplane window.

"Me too," he replied, not picking up on her detached nonverbals. "I travel for work pretty often. How about you?"

"Not too often."

"I work for a company that makes private jets. I fly back and forth between Florida and the Northeast pretty often. You work full time?" Her friendly, nosy neighbor wore khaki pants, a baby-blue golf polo, and a navy sweater vest. She considered telling him she wasn't in the mood for small talk, but he seemed kind, so she dismissed the idea. Whenever people inquired about her work, she felt an odd bit of shame that welled up, a need to justify herself in light of the inheritance secret she kept.

"Yes. Well, I actually have two part-time jobs. I'm an adjunct professor at a university in Orlando, and I'm a writer."

"Wow—that's great! You actually have published books, or are you one of these aspiring writers?"

"Yes, I have four published books—middle-school novels."

"You really are the real deal! Who knew, I'm sitting next to an author! I'm always glad to meet hardworking people. In my work, I encounter a lot of these entitled trust-fund babies. You know, these are the types that want the private jets. My cousin Jeff, his wife is that way too, never had to work for anything in her life—had everything just handed to her. It's hard to have any respect for people like that, you know? They have no idea about real life or what it's like to go through hard times."

Campbell continued looking outside her window. She thought about giving him a piece of her mind: "Hard times? Let me tell you about hard times. My father died when I was in college. My mom tries to take advantage of me every chance she gets. My brother is lying in a hospital bed, barely holding onto life after overdosing because the charmed life isn't always easy. I've had to fight for respect all my life from people in financial offices, at work, and on airplanes who would rather hold onto resentment than try to understand that for everyone, nothing comes without a cost—not even a trust fund.

The old Campbell would have spouted off at him without thinking. She credited Russ for teaching her to think before speaking. He had a way of responding, rather than reacting, and it had rubbed off on her. Despite the strong emotion stirring inside her, she decided that she didn't have the energy to take on the unsuspecting man in the sweater vest. On the other hand, she hated the sentiment underneath his misunderstandings.

She took a deep breath and smiled genuinely. "Your cousin's wife—does she work?"

"No! Never worked a day in her life! I think she passes her time up at the church, teaching English to foreigners and working in the nursery with the babies."

"Well, it sounds to me like she works—she's just not getting paid! I'll tell you, I have twins. They're older now, but when they were babies or toddlers, those volunteers working in the church nursery were my sanity. Just to get an hour or two of adult conversation at my moms' group was an enormous blessing. I'm grateful there are people, no matter what their financial situation, that give their time to others. We could use more of that these days. I'm trying to let go of my stereotypes about specific groups of people and take each person at face value, because you never know what people are going through, you know?"

The man seemed surprised by her response, given that she hadn't said more than five words to him previously in the conversation. "Hmmm, I guess I hadn't thought about it like that."

Campbell reached into the canvas bag under the seat in front of her and pulled out her laptop.

"You working on a book right now?" He continued to pry.

"Yes."

"I'll leave you to your craft, then. My name's Bill Gardner, by the way."

"Thank you. I'm…Lane Brock," she lied to keep him from successfully Googling her.

The plane landed and Campbell eventually managed to lose Bill Gardner, who trailed her from the gate down to baggage claim. She rented a car at the airport and made her way to the same hospital downtown where she visited her dying father so many years ago.

Tyler had contacted Debbie, who had picked him up and driven him to the hospital after the ambulance drivers refused to let him ride along. Her involvement in Cole and Tyler's life was minimal since Cole and Campbell had moved her into her condo.

Campbell texted her nephew, who met her at the ground-floor elevators of the hospital. The elevator doors opened to reveal a lanky boy wearing skinny jeans and a T-shirt, with straight blond hair that flopped down into his eyes. When she saw him, she wrapped him in a tight hug that he half-heartedly returned.

"Hi, buddy, glad to see you, but not like this. You doing okay? Have you been in to see your dad?"

"Yeah, he's still not awake. They're pumping his stomach, which is pretty gross."

She wrapped her arms around her nephew. "Okay, I'm here now. Everything's going to be okay. Where's Grandma?"

"She left. She said she had to go to some meeting for the Humane Society Charity Ball that she's helping Mrs. Newberry plan."

"Unbelievable. Her son's in the hospital, and she leaves her teenage grandson to fend for himself at the hospital!" Campbell spoke without thinking and then regretted sharing her anger in front of Tyler.

"She said she was really sorry, but whatever."

As they made their way through the door to Cole's hospital room, Campbell caught sight of her brother, a variety tubes coming out of his body. A flood of anger, pity, and fear surged through her body. Tyler immersed himself in his phone while Campbell sat waiting for her brother to gain consciousness so she could find out if there were any lasting effects from his overdose. She heard a doctor inquire about Cole's condition from the nurse's desk across the hall, and went over to get some information.

"I'm sorry, ma'am. Because of HIPPA laws, we are not able to share any information about your brother's condition unless he gives us consent."

"He's unconscious—he can't provide consent. Can't you just tell me if he's going to be okay?"

"All I can tell you is that he is in the process of being admitted to the hospital. We expect that he'll regain consciousness within the next couple of hours. I'm sorry I can't offer more information. His social worker is on his way up here. She will probably want to get some history from you."

"So you can't give me any information, but you want me to tell you everything I know."

"I know this is difficult. I'm very sorry." The doctor turned and walked down the hallway.

An hour later, the social worker, a compassionate woman in her early sixties with brilliant white hair, met Campbell in the waiting room and escorted her to an office on the main floor of the hospital. After gathering a family history and information about Cole's drug and alcohol use, she began asking questions about Tyler.

"The first responders said that there was a teenager present in the home with your brother and no other adults living in the home. Is that correct?"

"Yes. He had a nanny living with them, but I learned today that she was recently fired."

"And the dispatcher noted that Tyler said there had been cocaine and pills in the home. Were you aware of this?"

"No. I wasn't."

"And how old is your nephew?"

"He'll be sixteen in a couple months."

"What support people are in his life that can care for him while his father is recovering?"

"Um, just me, really. His grandmother lives locally, but she isn't very reliable."

"Where is the boy's mother?"

"She's never been a part of his life. My brother has had full custody since Tyler was a baby."

"I see," the woman replied, looking for options. "And you live out of state?"

"I mean, I'll be staying with Tyler for now, until Cole is back on his feet."

She put down her pen and clipboard on the side table that sat between their chairs. "You do understand that could be a long time. I can't speak about your brother's situation directly due to HIPPA laws, but patients in his condition typically recover here for a few days and are then transferred to another inpatient facility for thirty days or more. Are you prepared to care for Tyler for that length of time?"

"I guess I hadn't thought it through completely, but I'll do whatever it takes to care for Tyler until my brother is back on his feet."

"Given the history you've provided about your brother's drug use, I would suggest you consider a plan B. I'd like to stay hopeful that your brother will go willingly to rehab and come out at the end of four weeks ready to ditch the drugs and get back to responsibly caring for his son. If that doesn't happen, it would be wise to have a plan already in place to minimize the negative impact on the boy."

"Okay. A plan B. I believe I am the plan B. And, as I mentioned, I live out of state, so I'll have to think about this."

"You may want to consider contacting a lawyer."

"Okay. I'll do that now. Thank you."

"You can go up to see your brother now. I was just at the nurses' station and they said he's waking up."

Tyler sat in the waiting room, headphone wires hanging from his ears, eyes fixed downward on his iPhone. Walking toward him, Campbell caught his eye and motioned for him to come to the elevators. He slowly, defiantly, shook his head left and right and then returned to the game he was playing on his phone.

Campbell walked over and stood in front of him. "Tyler, your dad's waking up. You want to go see him?"

"Nope."

"Okay. I get that, I guess. Are you all right sitting here? I'd like to go see how he's doing."

"Whatever."

"Just text me if you need me, okay?"

Tyler never looked up from his phone, thumbs playing a drumbeat of anger, firing gunshots at realistic-looking zombies. She turned toward the elevators, her stomach tied in knots as she thought of her brother lying in the hospital bed upstairs, tubes coming out of all parts of his body, the broken shell of the man that couldn't seem to find his way out of the dark hole he had dug for himself. She struggled to understand how he would emerge, physically or emotionally, from being so broken. He had lost the business and he had lost his connection with his son, who wouldn't even see him. She desperately hoped that he hadn't lost any of his physical capacities from the overdose, and since she wasn't sure if the overdose had been accidental or a suicide attempt, she worried he had lost his will to live.

His eyes were closed as she walked quietly up to his bed. Relieved, she noticed his breathing tube had been removed. She gently grabbed his hand and watched his eyes crack open and take in her presence.

He mouthed, "Cammie," but no sound emerged from his dry, painful throat.

All of her anger stepped aside for a moment as gratitude and compassion rose in her heart. "Hey there, big brother. I'm glad to see you're still here in the land of the living. The nurses said you could have some ice chips. You want some?"

He nodded his head gratefully, and Campbell fell right back into her caregiving role.

"Where's Tyler?" Cole uttered the first words that offered her reassurance that he was at least healthy enough to be concerned for his son.

"He's downstairs in the waiting room, blaring angry music into his ears. It's fair to say that you've got some repair work to do with him."

"Yeah. I'm no good for him."

"You're his dad, Cole. He needs you to step up and get it together."

Cole looked down at his struggling body—IV, catheter, stomach tube. "He doesn't need me like this. If I keep screwing him over like this, he's gonna end up just like me. You should...just take him for a while. Get him outta here."

"They said you'll be in the hospital for a few days, and then they want to transfer you to a rehab facility. So I was planning to just stay here with Tyler at your house until you can..."

Cole carefully shook his head no and continued to speak in a forced whisper. "I've disrupted everyone's life enough. He needs something more stable. I don't want him to see me like this. Don't let him come up here. Pack him up and move him down to Florida with you. I mean today. Have my assistant write whatever checks you need to get him enrolled in the twins' school and set up to live a normal life with you guys. Have the lawyers draft the paperwork to give you custody until I get my shit together."

His words confirmed to Campbell the depth of the darkness Cole was facing. "Cole..."

"Just do it, Cam."

"Cole, I—"

"I appreciate that you came here and helped Tyler through this, but I don't want you here. I made this mess. I'll clean it up on my own."

"I can help you, Cole."

"You are helping me. Just get Tyler out of here. And there's nothing you can do to help me. That's what the doctors and nurses are for. Please. Just go."

"I want to help you get better. You can get over this, Cole. We'll get you back on track."

Cole closed his eyes and ignored her pleading.

Conflicted and overwhelmed, Campbell's mind raced and anger rose inside her. How could he put her in this position? How could he put his son in this position? Left with few options, she acquiesced. "Okay. Will you call me when you can? At rehab, or after you get out? Please? In the meantime, I'm praying for you. That you'll have the strength you need to get better." Campbell lifted the spoon to offer her brother more ice chips.

He opened his eyes and looked directly into hers, raising his hand to decline the ice and her support. "Don't waste your prayers on me."

Campbell leaned over and hugged her brother tightly, too angry to cry, too scared to let him go. He accepted her hug for a moment and then pushed her back. "Go." She gathered her strength and released her broken brother. Grabbing her purse and turning around on her heel, she walked out of the room without looking back.

YOUR MEETING WITH LANE

1. Have you encountered people, like the man on the airplane with Campbell, that resentfully stereotype people who have wealth or inherited money? What motivates their resentment? In what way are these stereotypes true or false?

2. Should people who have received inherited money hide this fact from others? Why or why not?

3. What is your opinion of Cole's decision to send Tyler to live with Campbell? What benefits might result? What problems might occur?

4. If you have experienced a similar situation in your family, where one family member had to pick up the responsibilities of another family member, discuss how this affected you individually and affected your family dynamics.

5. What concerns do you have about Cole and his ability to recover from this low point in his life?

1993

Final Moments

Death is not the greatest loss in life.
The greatest loss is what dies inside us while we live.
— *Norman Cousins*

Rays of morning sun cut through the tall cottonwood tree that adorned the front yard of the Hannigan house. Tucking the blanket tighter around her shoulders, Campbell rocked on the front porch swing, taking in the beauty of the glistening lake that stretched out across the street. Jim had moved into this house, which was far nicer than her modest childhood home, after Campbell started college. Over the past few weeks, she had no trouble settling into the space, which provided a beautiful setting for her to find peaceful moments of escape while caregiving for her dying father. Sometimes she just needed a break, and when Jim began to sleep frequently on and off throughout the day, she took brief moments of respite whenever she could.

Watching her father's health decline during his last weeks of fighting cancer was nearly too much for her to bear. She glanced down at the baby monitor, which allowed her the freedom to go outside or upstairs for brief periods of time while still being available if her father should need her. In the past week, Campbell had begun sleeping in the king bed adjacent to her father's hospital bed in the master bedroom. Because of his medications, Jim had to use the bathroom several times throughout the night, and his gait had become too unsteady to go alone. The neurologist concluded that the tumor in his brain had grown and was now severely affecting his balance and coordination, so he required assistance when standing or walking. Campbell was exhausted in ways she had never experienced, but her resolve never faltered. She had committed to caring for her father, and she anticipated that role would become even more challenging in the weeks to come.

At Jim's last oncology appointment, the doctor had recommended that hospice nurses begin making visits to the house. Campbell checked her watch. The hospice team would arrive for their first home meeting in thirty minutes. Her mind darted to Cole. She had called to invite him to attend, and surprisingly, he had agreed to come. Cole's visits had been less frequent in the past weeks. It seemed too difficult for him to see his father, a man full of strength, intellect, and charm, failing in all his capacities.

"I should call Cole to remind him about the meeting," Campbell thought to herself. She left the front porch and walked into the library to retrieve the portable phone. As she dialed the numbers and shared the reminder with her brother, she found herself distracted by something across the room that had caught her eye. A fluttering movement from the sill of the library's large picture window called to her. She said goodbye to her brother and walked over to the window. Getting a closer look, she discovered a mourning cloak butterfly with yellow tipped wings, weak and struggling to fly, frustrated by the window pane blocking its access to the outdoors. Campbell crouched down and watched it for a moment, wondering what she could do to help it. She figured this butterfly must have been hibernating somewhere in the house and had awoken, confused, when the heat in the house had recently been turned on at the end of an unseasonably warm fall. There was great determination in its wings, but it simply lacked the physical strength to take flight. A strong need to save the creature welled up inside of Campbell. She couldn't sit and watch the struggle any longer, so she went into the kitchen, soaked a sponge with honey-infused water and sliced an orange. Slowly, carefully, she placed the nourishment on the window sill next to the butterfly.

"Keep fighting, Mr. Butterfly," Campbell whispered. The butterfly fell over on its side. Her throat tightened, fighting unexpected tears, but she swallowed the sentiment down, feeling embarrassed about being emotional over something so silly.

The meeting with hospice came and went, leaving Campbell with a sense of reassurance in having the extra support for the difficult weeks to come. Cole seemed distant and overwhelmed by the information the team shared with them. When the nurses offered their opinion that Jim was likely entering his final days, Cole had left the room. After the meeting ended, Campbell found him sitting out on the porch swing.

"Are you okay?"

"Yeah. I just didn't want to be in there listening to them share the details of how his body will be breaking down."

"Well, I need to know all of that so I know how to take care of him, and what to expect."

"Aren't you scared, Cam?"

"I'm terrified, actually, but I mean, at least he gets to do this at home, in the most peaceful way possible. That's what he wants, right?"

"I give you a lot of credit."

Campbell smiled with gratitude for his acknowledgment. "You know, he's awake. I just went to check on him. Why don't you go talk to him? He'll be glad to see you."

With hesitation, Cole walked in to have what he feared might be his last conversation with his father. When he entered the room, he found his father with his eyes closed. For a moment, he worried, but then saw Jim's chest rising and falling sharply with each labored breath, even while he slept.

Cole sat down in the chair at his father's bedside. "Dad?" he whispered. No response. "So, I'm not sure if you can hear me, but I guess, I'll just talk to you anyway. I don't have a lot of time. There's a mess in the warehouse today, so I've got to get back to work. I guess the big shipment of parts that went out to Chrysler this week was faulty, every piece of it. I don't know what broke down on the quality-control side, but we've got to get it figured out because we have another big order they won't accept until we can offer some reassurance about what went wrong. If we lose Chrysler, we go under. I don't have to tell you that. I don't know how you handled all this pressure, Dad. And you never lost your cool with people. You handled it all so well. People really respect you...I respect you too. You were always such a great dad, and I love you for it." Cole squeezed his thumb and fingers sharply into the bridge of his nose between his eyes, pushing down the heaviness of the moment. "I'll do my best to make you proud."

Cole pushed down the emotion welling inside him and stood to his feet, firmly grabbing his father's limp right hand from the bedsheet in what would be their final handshake. Cole turned and walked out of the room without looking back. Grabbing his keys, he left the house without saying goodbye to his sister.

Throughout the evening, Campbell went back several times to the library to check on the butterfly, which remained alive, sitting upright, enjoying the plate of food. The nourishment and Campbell's care seemed to have awakened its vitality.

"Cammie, is it tomorrow that Lane is coming to meet with me?" Jim spoke slowly between spoon-fed bites of mashed potatoes. He hadn't eaten in two days, but when he'd unexpectedly asked for food, Campbell knew he would ask for mashed potatoes, his favorite. His frame was gaunt and frail, and just the effort to choose words and speak them seemed to require an inordinate amount of his depleted energy, so opportunities to talk with her father were becoming less frequent. They often just sat in silence together. Most of the time, his mind was in a distant place and it seemed to be a struggle for him to focus on the present moment. His movement had slowed drastically. In some ways, it felt to Campbell that the father she knew and loved was already gone, leaving just the failing shell of that man behind. Tonight, however, Jim had an unexpected burst of focus and energy.

"Yes. She'll be here early, 9 a.m. Do you want to get up and dressed before she comes, or just stay in bed?"

Jim thought for a moment, conflicted. "I'd like to get up, but I'm just not sure I've got the strength."

"She'll understand. We'll get you cleaned up, but there's no reason you can't have your meeting from the bed, if that's where you're most comfortable."

He looked at his daughter for a long moment, and then a soft smile formed across his mouth. He spoke again, slowly, thinking and breathing deliberately through his words. "People think that Cole is the strong one, but he is tough on the outside and soft on the inside. I found out, through all of this, that it's you—you're the strong one." He shook a thin finger in her direction "You're soft on the outside, but tough on the inside."

Campbell grabbed his hand and leaned in to listen closely, understanding that the thoughts he shared were treasured last words.

"There are some other things I need to say. Watch over Cole. You guys are going to need each other. If he falls down, you be there to pick him up. The two of you are all that's left of the Hannigans." Jim's mouth had become too dry to continue, so he motioned for water, which Campbell offered him; she guided the straw to his lips. After a couple of strained swallows, he continued, "Now one day, you and Cole might be blessed with children. Teach those kids to sail my boat, eh? Tell them all the reasons why I loved to go sailing. Make sure they know a thing or two about their Grandpa Jim. Use the money to leverage their strengths and passions, but be diligent to protect them from all the ways the money can hold them back. Stay connected to Lane; she seems to unlock the leader in you. Seek God, and maybe we'll all find ourselves reunited someday. Finally, thank you. Thank you, for walking with me down this dark road. You're a brave girl. I'm proud of you, and I know you're gonna be all right."

Campbell climbed up to lie in the bed, next to her father. She embraced him with a hug that was both gentle and fierce. "Thank you, Daddy. I'll keep your words in my heart forever."

After sharing this sacred moment, the evening and night that followed were their most difficult. In a great deal of pain, Jim took a dose of morphine that should have offered peaceful rest, but his breathing was so labored that, together, they struggled through the long hours of the night.

The next morning, Campbell greeted Lane and walked her down the hall toward the library to see the butterfly.

"He actually flew around the room a few times yesterday, so I think he's doing much better. I figure maybe if I keep feeding him, I can keep him alive through the winter and then release him when the weather warms in the spring."

When they entered the library, Campbell's heart sank. The butterfly lay flat on the floor underneath the window sill, its wings dull and gray. "Oh, dear." Lane placed a comforting hand on Campbell's shoulder.

Campbell had no words, but knelt down beside the butterfly and began to cry tears of exhaustion, disappointment over the butterfly and grief for her father. Normally stoic, Lane was so struck by the symbolism of this moment she brought Campbell to her feet and wrapped her in an embrace.

Pulling back, Campbell wiped her tears away with her hands. "I'm so sorry. I'm such a mess. I know it's not just about the butterfly, but I just really wanted to save it, you know?"

Lane put her hand around Campbell's waist and walked her out to the kitchen to get a glass of water. "I know you did. I know you did. You're a fixer, Campbell, just like your father. You cannot fix the things that are broken right now. Some experiences are defined by how well we learn to live in the midst of all the brokenness."

After pulling herself together with the help of Lane's encouragement, Campbell broke the news. "So, I mentioned that my dad had a really rough night last night. I wasn't sure he would even make it until the morning. I'm very sorry, but he said he can't meet with you this morning. He doesn't want you to see him like this. He asked for a pen and paper last night, and he wrote you a letter. I didn't read it, of course, but when I put it into the envelope, I saw that he could just barely write the words, so I hope you can read it." Campbell passed the sealed white envelope to Lane.

"Thank you. May I have a moment?" Lane asked.

"Of course. I need to get back there and check on him anyway." Campbell made her way to her father while Lane got settled at the kitchen table and opened the letter.

Dear Lane,

First, thank you for the vital role you have taken in my life and the kids' lives these last few months. I hate to think of the opportunities I would have missed and poor decisions I might have made without your guidance and insight during this difficult time. Because of our sessions, I have been more thoughtful in my estate planning, more circumspect about the business succession plan, and more generous with my giving, and I have made the most of the limited time with my children. Most importantly, I am making my exit being intentional about the legacy I leave behind. I believe these lessons will have an immeasurable impact on the Hannigan family for generations.

I really hope my death does not mark the end of your relationship with my family. I have made specific direction to allow for my estate to pay your fees should Cole and Campbell agree to continue working with you. They will, no doubt, face many challenges in the months to come that may require your assistance, but I hope you'll still be working with them even decades from now.

I had the most vivid dream yesterday. You were holding a meeting at Sears Tower in Chicago. Campbell and Cole were there with their adult children and what must have been nearly a dozen younger children. Everything was good. They were healthy and happy, and I had the sense that they all really had their act together. The odd part was, you had planned the meeting, but you weren't facilitating the meeting, you were with me, floating outside the window looking in. Must be all the morphine making me loopy! I don't know what that dream means, Lane, but I loved what I saw, and I desperately want that vision to become a reality. There won't be much I can do to make that happen after I'm gone, but I'm betting that with you continuing to serve as a trusted advisor, they will all be much better prepared for what lies ahead.

Lane, I do hope you know...the work you do changes lives and impacts families for generations.

Going with Gratitude,

Jim Hannigan

Lane let his words and all the sentiment behind them roll around in her mind. In her field, she often worked with terminal patients. She was no stranger to death or grief. You might say she specialized in helping others face the reality of their death, and sometimes that meant that she walked with them right to the end. She took a deep breath and admitted to herself that no other family had impacted her like the Hannigans, although she couldn't allow her emotions to confuse her professional responsibility to them. Defiantly, she swallowed back her tears, arose from the table, and walked into the kitchen to place her cup into the dishwasher. Drying her hands on the towel that hung from the stove handle, Lane's heart sank as she saw Campbell walk into the kitchen, expressionless.

"He's gone, Lane. My dad's gone."

YOUR MEETING WITH LANE

1. What did Campbell learn from her serendipitous experience with the butterfly?

2. What did you think of the final words Jim chose to share with Campbell? In what ways did his values change between when he was diagnosed and when he died?

3. Imagine a moment where you have the opportunity to share parting words with a specific loved one before you die. What would you say?

4. Cole did not have the opportunity to have a final conversation with Jim before he died, but he did get to share some of his own sentiments while Jim slept. If Jim had been awake, do you think Cole would have shared the same thoughts? Why or why not? If so, what might Jim have said in response to what Cole had shared?

2015

The Fear That You'll Fall

Let me fall.
Do not stop me from falling.
Just be there to help me get up if I need you.
— Sima Mittal

"I'll be right back. I'm going to get help, Dad. Don't fall. I have to leave, but please don't fall. No, No!"

"Cam, wake up. Wake up. Baby, you're dreaming."

Campbell sprung up in the bed, covered in sweat.

"Oh, Russ. I was having this awful dream. My dad was standing on the edge of this cliff. He was in pain, hunched over. I had to leave to go get help. I knew that as soon as I turned around, he would fall. As you woke me, I heard him slipping, but when I turned around, it wasn't my dad anymore, it was Cole who was falling. All I could do was stand there and watch him fall. There was nothing I could do."

"Come here." Russ laid her back down, wrapped her in his arms, and they lay silent together for a few moments. "Cam, you have left a serious sweat shadow in this bed.

223

Maybe we should move over to my side." They both giggled, and Russ felt her body relaxing. "You know, you have these dreams about your dad a lot. It's always like he needs your help somehow, and something happens where you miss your chance to help him."

"Yeah. You're right. I do. They're terrible dreams."

"I wasn't around in those tough days when you were taking care of him at the end. It couldn't have been easy, and I know it bothers you that you weren't sitting right there with him when he passed. But, Campbell, maybe it all happened just like it was supposed to, like your dad wanted it to happen."

"What do you mean?"

"Well, I've heard you say your dad hated the fact that you had to leave college and go through all the hardships of caring for him, especially having to see him like that. Seems he was very protective of you. Have you ever thought that maybe you missed the moment your dad died, not because you were some neglectful caregiver off talking with Lane, but because your dad didn't want to leave you with that difficult last moment? He was an independent man! I bet he hated having to lean on you like that. This may have been his final show of independence and protection of his baby girl."

Her silence made Russ second-guess the candor with which he had addressed this sensitive subject.

When Campbell finally spoke, her voice quivered with emotion. "It's like you know him so well, and you never even met him."

"Aw, I know him. He is Cole's intensity and womanizing ways. He's your stubbornness and creativity. He is Jade's math skills and Jimmie's photographic memory. He's Tyler's face and mannerisms and courage. And I think it's no mistake that crazy mind of yours turned your dad into Cole in the dream, because you're doing the same thing with your brother. Taking on too much responsibility for other people. You're worried he's gonna fall off the wagon and start using drugs again."

Campbell giggled and turned to look at her husband. "How much do I owe you for this therapy session?"

"Hey, I like the sound of that," he replied, rubbing his hands across her waist.

"But you'll have to bill me." Detaching from his grip, Campbell swung her legs off the edge of the bed and sat up.

Russ protested from his pillow. "Hey, where are you going?"

"I'm sorry. You gave me a lot to think about. I feel like I need to sit down and write for a while."

"All right, but if you change your mind about wantin' to pay that bill, you know where I'll be."

Campbell threw her pillow playfully at him and walked into the kitchen to pour herself a glass of water. She sat down at the computer, which signaled ten new emails. After sorting through them, she opened Facebook and began scrolling the news feed. A few minutes in, a tiny sound signaled a new chat message.

Cole: Hey, Sis. What are you doing up in the middle of the night?

Campbell: I suppose I could ask the same of you. You okay?

Cole: I'm not sure how to answer that.

Campbell: Are you drunk/high Cole? You know I told

you when you were here for Tyler's graduation, we don't want any contact with you when you're like that!

Cole: Easy, Sis! No, I'm completely sober. Sober forty-two days actually!

Campbell: I'm sorry for assuming. That's great. I'm really proud of you. Having trouble sleeping?

Cole: As usual. Used to be the drugs amping me up that kept me from sleep. Now it's regrets.

Cole: It's the worst part of getting clean actually. You'd think the detox would be the worst—yeah, that was pretty awful too—but the hardest thing about being sober is that you have all these stupid mistakes you made, people you hurt, opportunities you lost staring back at you every time you close your eyes. And then you don't even have the drugs to numb the pain of all that.

Campbell: I'm not sure what to say…

Campbell: Except that—I think what you're doing, getting clean, is really brave. I'm sure it's not easy. But at the same time, you should know that I feel apprehensive to let you in and to get all excited about your sobriety, because I'm not sure I can handle the disappointment if it falls apart again. After you lost the business and said you were done using, we believed you, and I don't think you even tried to quit. After your overdose, when we took custody of Tyler and you finally started counseling, it was only a couple months before you were back at it again. It breaks my heart every time. I just can't ride that rollercoaster anymore.

Cole: I get it. And I know I can't convince you, but this time, it's different. I have some things I need to say to you, and I hope it's okay to say them in writing this way instead of in person. You know I've never been good at that.

Cole: I don't know how to say I'm sorry to you, Campbell. Or to let you know how grateful I am for the ways you stepped up to help me and Tyler. But I am so sorry. I'm sorry for losing our family business. I'm sorry for not appreciating the incredible sister that you are. I'm sorry you have to raise my kid because I'm such a screwup. I'm sorry I ruined the graduation party you gave him. I'm sorry for all the times I've embarrassed you or let you down.

His words sat in her mind like a coveted gift waiting to be unwrapped. She simply didn't have the courage to unwrap his sentiments and allow them into her heart, for fear that they would be ripped back one day. Still, she knew that holding onto resentment toward her brother did no one any good. A silent debate raged in her heart and mind, opposing sentiments making their case to let him in, or guard her heart. She was ready to forgive, but reluctant to open her heart back up to him after so many disappointments.

Campbell: I have to admit that I don't trust you yet… but I forgive you.

Cole: I get it. I know I can't erase the hurt that I've caused you and Tyler and everyone else. I just want to get back on the right path.

Campbell: I want that for you too.

Cole: I have been going to a psychiatrist and a counselor. They've diagnosed me with generalized anxiety disorder and explained that I've been self-medicating my anxiety with drugs and alcohol. I'm learning how to recognize my anxiety and work through it in healthier ways. I worry about so much, Campbell. I always have. After Dad died, I was so worried about screwing everything up, losing the business. Ironically, all that worry actually drove me right into failure.

Campbell: I'm sorry I could never help you with it. I always saw your anxiety. I just didn't know how to help.

Cole: It's not your fault. I didn't know how to help me either.

Campbell: I've always wondered—and it's okay if you feel this is too private to share with me— what did Dad write in the letter he wrote to you that night before he died?

Cole: It's funny you should ask that.

Campbell: Why?

Cole: Well, because I couldn't have answered that question until last week.

Campbell: What do you mean?

Cole: Because I didn't read it until last week

Campbell: You never read Dad's letter until last week??? It's been over 20 years, Cole! Weren't you so curious about what it said?

Cole: I just couldn't bring myself to open it. I had trouble even thinking about Dad's death. I knew the letter would bring a flood of feelings I couldn't handle. It's been haunting me from the drawer of my bedside table unopened all these years, but I just couldn't do it.

Campbell: Wow. Ok. Well....what did it say?

Campbell: Hello???

Cole: I think I'd like to keep it between Dad and I, but I will tell you that not reading the letter back then was the biggest mistake of my life.

Campbell: Oh, you are killing me. I've never been more curious about anything in my life!

Cole: It's enough to say that it would have taken a lot of pressure off my shoulders to read it when I was struggling to fill his shoes running the business. Even reading it now has been very healing for me.

Campbell: You'd better sleep with one eye open because if I get my hands on that letter, I'm totally reading it!

Cole: You really should have been a private investigator. I bet Tyler gets away with nothing living in your house!

Campbell: Is it wrong that this makes me feel proud? Seriously though, I'm really happy you read the letter and that it brought you some peace.

Cole: It definitely did. So in other news, I've decided to start a little business venture. Since I lost the business, I've spent a lot of time out on my boat. Dad was right—being out on the water is good for the soul. Anyway, it started pissing me off how much pollution is out on the water, so I went home and started fiddling around with some ideas on paper, and I think I've got a pretty innovative idea. I had lunch with a retired engineer yesterday, and he thought it was such a viable idea he offered to invest! I suppose I could live off my inheritance without working, but I've got too much energy, and the extra time on my hands isn't a good thing. I talked to Jack about it too, and he says he thinks it's worth pursuing. I need feedback from the people closest to me about things like this because I'm afraid to trust myself. As you know, I haven't always made the best decisions in the past.

Campbell: Sounds exciting. Definitely something worth pursuing!

Cole: It feels good to think about making something on my own, especially something that will make a difference in the world.

Campbell: Who knows, maybe this will become a business Tyler would be interested in. He's very eco-minded, and in some environmental club at the college.

Cole: I just want Tyler to figure out who he is and what he loves to do.

Campbell: My heart is full.

Cole: Why?

Campbell: Cole, I've prayed for you for years—decades actually. Sometimes, I didn't even know who I was praying to, or for what, but I was desperate to help you. And now you're getting your life back on track and making some really good decisions. I'm so happy for you.

Cole: I suppose only God himself could change a dope like me. I'm still living at Jack's house, and he's got me going to church with them every Sunday. It's all making a lot of sense to me. It's like I have a hunger for meaning inside me now. I've wasted so much of my life on things that don't even matter. I've always worried (I know, more anxiety) that I'll die young like Dad. You know, what if it's genetic? Our great-grandmother on Dad's side died young too. I used to think, I better live hard and party it up because I'm going to die young anyway. Now I think, I want to use whatever time I have left to make the most of the present moment, to connect with Tyler and with you guys, and do something meaningful with my life. That's why I'm pouring my heart out to you in the middle of the night. I really miss you, Cam.

Campbell: I miss you too.

Cole: All right, you better get your butt to bed. Don't you have three teenagers to clean up after all day tomorrow?

Campbell: Yes! Tyler Hannigan, in particular. I love that boy desperately, but being raised with a maid was not good for him.

Cole: Whoops. What were we supposed to do, clean that enormous house ourselves? Trust me, that would have been worse.

Campbell: I dunno, maybe teach the kid clean up after himself? I always know what he's been doing after he gets home because he leaves a trail of mess behind him wherever he goes.

Cole: Funny, Jack's wife said the same thing about me since I've been living here at their house.

Campbell: Like father, like son. ;)

Cole: No way. Tyler will turn out way better than me. His Aunt Campbell is raising him, and she's relentless.

Campbell: You've always known how to sweet talk me, Big Brother.

Cole: Goodnight, Cam.

Campbell: Goodnight, Cole.

YOUR MEETING WITH LANE

Sometimes we'll never get a beautiful apology, like Cole's words to Campbell, from those who have hurt us. This lack of acknowledgment can make it easy to hold onto bitterness, but that resentment serves only to hold us back.

1. Looking back over your life, what are your regrets? Whom have you hurt or disappointed? What relationship might benefit from an acknowledgement of and apology for your mistakes?

2. Looking back over your life, what areas of resentment toward others remain in your heart? What can you do to let go of that resentment and forgive?

3. Campbell recognized that maybe she could choose to forgive her brother, even though she still felt apprehensive to let him into her heart and fully trust him. Why might it be wise for Campbell to guard her heart, even with her brother's increasing success in sobriety? With what relationship in your life have you had to make a similar choice?

4. Campbell felt responsible for not being with her father at the moment he died, and she struggled to separate herself from her worries about her brother. In what ways do you overburden yourself with your loved ones' problems, causing undue stress? What challenges does this create for you? Where is the line between being caring and taking on more than your share of the burden?

2016

A Conversation with Teenagers

*I believe that what we become depends on
what our fathers teach us at odd moments,
when they aren't trying to teach us.
We are formed by little scraps of wisdom.*
—*Umberto Eco,* Foucault's Pendulum

Campbell Hannigan-Wilburn: Hi family, this is your text reminder that we have a family meeting tomorrow night at 6 p.m. out on the porch. Unless you have a broken limb, you are expected to be there. No excuses! And please confirm that you got this message.

Jade Wilburn: Yep. Got it. And, Mom, can we please go shopping for my prom dress after school today?

Jimmie Wilburn: Is it wrong that I'm seriously weighing breaking a limb vs. going to the family meeting?

Campbell Hannigan-Wilburn: Yes to shopping after school, Jade. No to broken limbs, Jimmie!

Russ Wilburn: I have a meeting tomorrow night, but I think I can move it to earlier in the day.

Campbell Hannigan-Wilburn: Best. Husband. Ever. Love you, babe! ♥

Jimmie Wilburn: Gross. Please don't send love emojis to Dad when we're all listening.

Jade Wilburn: I saw this amazing Valentino dress online that I love.

Campbell Hannigan-Wilburn: Valentino?!? Keep dreaming! We're really more of a Nordstrom Rack kind of family.

Russ Hannigan: This is your senior prom, not the red carpet.

Jimmie Wilburn: Can you guys take this fashion news update outside of the group message? I'm trying to study.

Tyler Hannigan: This family is hilarious.

Campbell Hannigan-Wilburn: Hi, Tyler. I hope you can make it to the family meeting tomorrow too?

Tyler Hannigan: Yep, I'll be there. Aunt Cam, can you confirm the date of the big annual meeting when my dad and all the financial people are coming to town?

Campbell Hannigan-Wilburn: Yes, thank you for bringing that to everyone's attention. It's at noon, two weeks from Saturday. Make sure you mark your calendars. I'm excited to see your dad. Sounds like he's doing great!

Tyler Hannigan: Yeah, I talked to him a couple days ago. He said he's been totally clean for nine months. He's being really cool with me...interested in what I'm doing and_everything. He even asked if I wanted to come up there on my break and stay with him.

Jade Wilburn: Will the investment people from NY be bringing the same intern to the annual meeting that they brought along last time? He was smokin' hot!

Russ Wilburn: Campbell, can you please confirm that the smokin' hot intern will NOT be present at the annual meeting?

Campbell Hannigan-Wilburn: I'm on it, Russ. And, kids, Lane said she has something really fun planned for you guys this year. I'll attach the agenda below. Please open it and read it before the meeting. Don't forget to bring your info to share about how you gave your money away for the Generosity Challenge this year and finish reading the book Uncle Cole recommended. Russ Wilburn, I know you aren't anywhere near finished!

Russ Wilburn: Will you read it to me tonight? You know I hate reading.

Jimmie Wilburn: Dad, I read the book and wrote a paper on it for class. If you want, you can just read my paper to save yourself some time.

Russ Wilburn: That's my boy!

Campbell Wilburn: Oh for heaven's sake, Russell Wilburn! Okay, I'm heading in to teach my afternoon class. Love you all!

Hannigan Annual Meeting Agenda

MORNING

Welcome

Family Values Activity

Leadership Development Book Discussion

Family Foundation Meeting

Financial Markets Overview

—LUNCH BREAK—

AFTERNOON

Adults and Children Split

Children: Budgeting and Online Accounting

Adults: Investment Performance Review,

Tax/Estate Planning Review

Closing

YOUR MEETING WITH LANE

Coordinating family meetings can be challenging with the harried pace of life, conflicting schedules, and complaining teenagers. This scheduled time, however, can be an important means to strategically invest financial, intellectual, human, social, and spiritual capital in your family.

1. If you have children still living at home, has your nuclear family considered holding weekly/monthly family meetings to coordinate schedules and connect around family successes or challenges? What hurdles might you face in trying to make these meetings a reality? In what specific ways might this kind of strategic meeting benefit your family? What problems are occurring currently in your family that might be improved as a result of having regular family meetings?

2. Has your extended family considered holding multigenerational annual meetings, perhaps concurrent with annual financial review meetings, to highlight important family values, celebrate family successes, and discuss important family business items? What hurdles might you face in trying to make these meetings a reality? In what specific ways might this kind of strategic meeting benefit your family? What problems are occurring currently in your family that might be improved by having regular family meetings?

2033

The Great Relay Race of Life

Life isn't a race. It's a relay.
—Dick Gregory

She paid the driver and wheeled her suitcase along the walkway to the front door of Campbell's Florida home. Lane never expected she'd still be traveling for client meetings at nearly seventy-five years old, but she would always make an exception for her favorite client. It had been a privilege to watch the once young and overwhelmed Campbell mature into a wise and respectable woman.

"What a gorgeous morning," Lane noted as the two strolled through Campbell's neighborhood, a canopy of oak trees providing shade from the Florida sun. "Can you believe next week will mark forty years since your father's passing?"

"It's impossible to believe that it's been so long. How did we get so very old, Lane?"

"If you're old, my dear, then I am an antique! I guess that marks the anniversary of our work together then too, doesn't it? It's certainly been my life's pleasure working with you and your family."

"Oh, stop it, Lane! I don't know where I'd be without your wisdom throughout my life."

"I expect you've had a good bit of time to reflect upon your life as you've been working on the book. I'm curious what you've learned as you've been writing down your life in story form."

"It's certainly been an eye-opening experience. There's a theme I watched emerge as the chapters built upon each other. I don't know why it surprised me, because it's exactly what you're always saying—it's what you've been helping me figure out my whole life. My story is about legacy. I sat watching a relay race at the grandkids' track meet one afternoon recently, and I had one of those sacred serendipity moments you're always talking about. Watching the girls and their friends run in a relay race, I began reflecting, and imagined myself and my family running a relay race together. I imagined my dad running an incredible race and then passing the baton to me, and to Cole, much earlier than we expected to receive it."

"You and your brother certainly were much too young to shoulder such responsibility," Lane interjected.

Campbell shot Lane a knowing smile and continued, "And then I asked myself, what motivates us to run? For my granddaughters running the track meet, they were trying to win the race, of course. I believe my father was similarly motivated by the idea of competing against the industry and against the high standards he held for himself. But what motivates the race for Cole and me? When I was younger, the thing that drove me was this neurotic fear that I would lose ground on all that my father had gained and passed on from his hard work. And Cole says he got so sick of worrying about dropping the baton, and the sheer weight of it, that he finally threw it down in defiance when he lost the business and fell headlong into his addictions. Both of us were running, not to win, but to avoid screwing it all up. What kind of sick motivation is that? No wonder we've both had our problems."

"You've made some powerful insights, Campbell."

"Thankfully, I've finally worked through some of that, and what a blessing it's been to watch Cole pick his baton up off the ground and run with his own sense of purpose."

"I'm so glad to hear he's doing well." Lane smiled fondly and Campbell continued.

"As I've gotten older, I've realized that my tight grip on that baton was actually holding me back from leveraging the financial capital my father invested in me. The real tragedy isn't in dropping the baton, but in allowing fear to keep me from running my own best race. Through these insights, I found a pace that focuses less on the baton and much more on improving my form and embracing the pure joy of running my own best leg of the race." Campbell thrust her arms back and forth as if she was running and smiled over at Lane, whose walking pace had now slowed a bit. Campbell motioned for the two to turn around and head back to the house as she continued talking.

"Now lately, I find myself thinking about how I'll pass off the baton to the kids, praying they'll make the transition and be equipped to run their best race, then pass the baton to their kids, and so on. We've got the benefit of the family members who ran before us. We know the stories about how they ran their races and we've all learned from each other, but I hope we've given them the courage and freedom to run their own leg of the race in their own beautiful way. I can see it all so clearly now, Lane." Rambling on and lost in her thoughts, Campbell looked up to find Lane with tears in her eyes.

"You, my dear, are the reason I do what I do." Lane stopped walking and pulled a tissue from her pants pocket, wiping the happy tears collecting at the bottom rim of her eyes. "Do you know that almost every known culture has a quote that cautions its successful families? 'Shirtsleeves to shirtsleeves in three generations.' Of course, in England we say, 'Clogs to clogs in three generations.' Campbell, you are working so hard to ensure that this won't be your family's destiny. I know in my heart that your legacy will most certainly continue to make a lasting, beneficial impact for generations to come, just as your father's legacy has."

"Thanks to you," Campbell deflected the compliment.

"And thanks to you," Lane pointed a finger bent with arthritis, "people across the world will have the opportunity to learn these lessons when they read your life story. I believe this book you've written will hit people in their hearts. The books I've authored have all the theory, the rhetoric, about wealth and legacy and the different types of capital, but your story—your story has the heart."

"I hope so. You know, I've always wondered, Lane, as you worked with my dad back then and the rest of us along the way, was there a step-by-step process you guided us through?"

"Yes and no. There are certain vital legacy concepts I

guide my clients to explore. I do have a written list of these, incidentally, but it's not truly a step-by-step process. Life lessons have a way of presenting themselves in their own serendipitous timing."

"Would you share your list of legacy concepts with me? I'd love to see it. It sort of sounds like your playbook!"

"Oh, I'd be glad to share it with you, dear."

"Can I include it in the appendix of the book?"

"Well, I can't see why not, if you think it would bring some benefit to your readers."

"Great. I do think will really help people."

Lane stopped walking, in part because all the talking was making her become a bit winded, but also because she wanted to drive home her next point. "Now, Campbell, I want to discuss this issue of you just handing over this book that you've written and asking me to put my name on the front cover. You've authored this story. I want you to get the credit for it! It's your story."

"And that's precisely why I'm asking you to put your name on it instead of mine. It's too personal. I think of all the questions I get asked about my middle-school novels at book signings or interviews for the local paper. I don't want to answer all those questions about this story. This is my life and it was important for me to write it all down, but I don't want to keep talking about it. I've changed the details so that no one will recognize it as the Hannigan story, so just tell people you wrote the book as a compilation of all your clients' life stories. Haven't you ever heard of a ghostwriter, Lane?" Campbell winked and put her arm around Lane as they finished their walk down the tree-canopied street.

Lane laughed, "You do remain stubborn as ever! A lot like your father, I might add!"

YOUR MEETING WITH LANE

Using Campbell's metaphor of a relay race, envision your own family across generations. As you reflect, consider the following questions:

1. Describe the race you see yourself running right now. If you are married, how does your spouse's pace differ from your own?

2. What traits of the those who ran before you in your family's race have inspired you and been incorporated into the way you approach your run?

3. What motivates you to keep running your best race?

4. What traits are you bringing to your part of the race that make it uniquely your own?

5. What strategic steps are you taking now to help prepare yourself and those to whom you will pass off the baton for this important transition?

6. Consider that moment when you will pass on the baton to the rising generation. How will you handle those first moments without the baton in your hand? How can you continue to contribute to the success of your family's race even after you pass the baton?

LANE'S LEGACY LIST

★ Educate yourself on research identifying the common negative impacts of wealth and study the habits of "100-year families" whose wealth beat the odds, surviving for generations.[1]

★ Invest strategically in the rising generation

★ Balance investments in each of the five areas: financial, intellectual, social, human, and spiritual. Consider that you might tend to overweigh investments in one or two areas.

★ Be mindful and open

★ Listen to the serendipitous lessons life is teaching and look for opportunities to share your story with the next generation.

★ Give rising generations age appropriate leadership roles.

★ Schedule weekly family meetings. Include children in annual family meetings and incorporate intentional, relevant learning processes into these meetings. Observe faith practices. Create traditions around spending time together.

★ Commit to teaching the next generation financial independence from an early age, even if it requires more time or trouble.

★ Teach financial literacy and financial independence. Encourage the next generation to establish relationships with your advisors. Strategically increase transparency about the family wealth, training them to understand the family's unique wealth landscape.

★ Allow those in the rising generation to run their own unique race.

★ Evaluate their strengths, note their passions, recognize that your way is not the only way, and help the next generation to maximize their unique impact and purpose.

★ Take a coach approach with the rising generation.

★ Ask more questions. Give fewer answers, with the goal of empowering heirs to function independently.

★ Take courageous inventory of yourself to define and maximize your intended legacy and to minimize any weaknesses that may undercut your goals.

★ Get involved in legacy coaching, emotional intelligence assessment, counseling, treatment of addictions, treatment of physical or mental illness, and so on.

★ Recognize that despite your best efforts to impart legacy values, you ultimately have limited control over the outcome of the lives of the next generation.

★ Money can buy many things, but it offers no guarantees in relationships. Exercise healthy boundaries in your relationships and get professional counseling to handle troubled relationships.

2034

That One Beautiful Chapter

*The greatest good you can do for another
is not just to share your riches, but to reveal to him his own.*
—*Benjamin Disraeli*

Every life story has that one dreaded chapter where it all falls apart, but for those who press on with determination, every life story also has that one beautiful chapter where it all comes together.

A racing heartbeat drowns out the sound of reality.

Boom—Boom—Boom.

All that once was scattered slips into place, and the whole world makes perfect sense, if even for a moment.

Her chapter began unexpectedly when she got the early-morning call to share the news that her lifelong mentor, Lane Brock, had died in her sleep the night before the Hannigan family's annual meeting. Campbell knew this moment would come, but her mentor's passing brought a heaviness to her chest that reminded her she was officially the oldest generation in her family. Of course, Lane hadn't been a blood relative, but over the years she had become like a grandmother to her children and like the supportive mother she had always desired.

Each member of the Hannigan family had loved and respected Lane in their own way. Campbell expected the annual meeting would be extremely challenging without Lane present, but she found that, even in death, Lane still offered such great wisdom.

The large conference room of the downtown Chicago hotel with its cherry-wood wainscot walls filled with chatter as Campbell's family members came in and found their seats. After everyone settled, Campbell rose to share the sad news about why Lane wouldn't be present. Before she opened her mouth, she looked around at each expectant face. Cole, with hair that had gone stately white, sat next to Tyler, a tanner version of his father at the same age, who sat next to his wife and four children. Russ and Campbell's children, Jade and Jimmie, sat with their spouses and six children between them. These eighteen individuals, related by blood or love, stirred such pride and affection in her. Twenty-five chairs in total sat around the large green marble table, some filled with investment managers, lawyers, and accountants, but the chair directly to Campbell's right sat conspicuously empty.

She cleared her throat, silently prayed the Breton Fisherman's Prayer, and began, "Thank you so much for your commitment to attending our annual family meeting. You may notice that there is someone missing from our meeting today. I received a call early this morning that Lane died in her sleep last night," she paused as her family reacted to the sad news, "after nearly eighty years of impacting the world around her in immeasurable ways. As you know, she's been slowing down, which is why we chose to have our annual meeting in Detroit this year so she didn't have to travel. Isn't it just like her to leave us just before our meeting, so we all would have the opportunity to use this time to talk about legacy?" Ever stalwart, Campbell cleared tenacious tears of grief from her throat. "I know she made a distinct impact upon each one of us, so the first item on the agenda this morning is to share some of our favorite memories of Lane. Who would like to begin?"

Jade's youngest son, six years old, raised his hand. "Mimi?"

Campbell smiled and took her seat. "Yes, Cooper. What do you remember about Lane?"

As he lowered his raised hand, a smile with several missing teeth spread across his face. "What I loved most about Lane is...the Jelly Babies! When Momma wasn't looking, she would always sneak us one or two of those gummy candies from her purse." The young boy looked tentatively at his mother. "She said the Jelly Babies were so good because the candy in England is way yummier than the kind you can get here in America."

"Yes, she did love her candy, didn't she?" Campbell replied with fondness.

Cooper's older cousin, Luke, agreed. "She didn't treat us like just kids. She talked to us like we were grown-ups, with respect. I really liked that."

Another cousin chimed in, "Yeah, like how she would always translate what the financial people said to us in, like, real person language." The young girl looked over to the financial team members around the table and apologized, "No offense."

Cole took his turn. "Through everything, Lane was always patient with me. When I gave her a hard time and refused to commit to her coaching, she never took it personally. She never gave up on me, and when I was finally ready to work with her, she never judged me. I wouldn't be the person I am today without her. I'm just sorry it took me so long to open myself up to her guidance."

Russ spoke next. "You know, people joke about how great it would be to marry someone with money, but it's actually really challenging. I think everyone around this table understands that." He looked over at Campbell and laughed along with the others. "Sorry, babe, you're an incredible wife, but you know it's true. Lane sat me down before we got married and talked to me about what to expect. With money, there can be a power differential. Some people might think that whoever has more money gets more decision-making power in the relationship. It doesn't have to be that way, and in fact, Campbell has never been that way. Lane helped us talk about money openly from even before our marriage, and set our foundation solid from the start by giving us a wedding gift of marriage counseling with one of her trusted colleagues. That's something we might not have done on our own, and I'm really grateful for all the wisdom Lane shared with Campbell before I met her and with both of us together throughout our lives."

Each family member took a turn to share. Then Campbell spoke again. "Thank you for all the beautiful words you each shared about Lane. It's amazing how one person can leave such a lasting, positive imprint on this world. We all leave an inheritance, even those who have no money at all. We leave an inheritance of our intellect, our spirit, our attitude, our approach to life, our sense of humor, our generosity, our faith, our interests, our passions, our wisdom, and our love. Some people, like our dear Lane, leave behind a beautiful inheritance. She's made each one of us better in incalculable ways. Lane taught me over and over again throughout my life to invest in spiritual capital. Whenever I was confused or searching for answers or unsure about a decision, she would never tell me what to do; instead, she encouraged me to be aware, to watch for what life was trying to teach me. She called it 'sacred serendipity.' Sure enough, every single time, some amazing coincidence would follow soon after. I hope each one of you will invest in spiritual capital. Create quiet moments, cultivate faith, grapple with the notion of God, make peace with unanswerable questions, find time for prayer, give generously, and keep your eyes wide open to notice moments of sacred serendipity. Invest deeply in this area of your life, and you will find your purpose in this world, you will make a difference in the lives of all those you encounter, and you will create a most beautiful legacy that will last for generations."

Campbell continued, "You all know that my journey with Lane began when Granddad Jim was diagnosed with cancer, just a few months before he died. I'm so grateful to him for hiring her and bringing her great insight to our family. Granddad Jim gave us Lane. He gave us the freedom of financial security and independence, but most importantly, he gave us a legacy of the values he held most dear. Cole embodies his work ethic and tenacity, and as you age, my dear brother, your whitening hair makes you look so remarkably like him. Sometimes when I'm with you, it's almost like I've been with him again. Thank you for that. Dad would be so proud of the way you've built your own eco-business from the ground, the way you've brought Tyler alongside you in the business, and of the respectable man you've become. You are so resilient, and I truly admire the legacy you are building with your life."

Campbell paused and looked around. "We are a pretty amazing family, aren't we? When Grandad Jim died, Cole and I were very young. We have done the best that we can, to honor his legacy and pass it down to all of you. Tyler, Jimmie, Jade, and spouses, you are each living your lives in ways that make us so proud. Let me encourage you: please don't try to run your race the same way we ran ours. Take what we learned from the generation above us, and then put that together with all that we've taught you, and use it to help guide you on your own path. And grandchildren, we are so excited to watch your lives unfold; you will always hear our voices cheering you along. Grandad Jim and our dear friend Lane have changed each one of us. Their legacies have made a powerful imprint on the three generations of people that sit in this one room, and I'm so grateful we were blessed to have had them in our lives."

Campbell would miss the vast majority of the business content that followed at that annual meeting, but she knew Russ would remind her of any essential items that required her follow-up. Distracted and emotional, Campbell juggled grief at the loss of Lane alongside delight at having the whole family together in her hometown. She snuck out of her meeting to peek at the grandchildren's meeting, their table littered with paper money and plastic coins. A younger consultant from Lane's office had been sent to facilitate the children's meeting. She watched the kids each hustling across the room with purpose, engaged in a simulated banking exercise. How proud her father would be to see his great-grandchildren getting smart about money. Could he somehow look down and see them carrying on his legacy, she wondered?

In that moment, the past, present, and future merged to create a beautiful mosaic in her mind. The Hannigan legacy certainly wasn't without its blemishes. Divorce, addiction, cancer, conflict, materialism, and more had threatened to tear them apart, and she knew there would be other hard times to come, but as she watched three generations of Hannigans gathered in a strategic effort to maximize the positive impact of their lives, all the pieces of their family legacy, the beauty and the tragedy, merged together in her mind, with heartbreaking beauty.

"Mimi, look!" Campbell looked down to see her youngest granddaughter jumping up and down, waving her artwork up high.

"What's this, honey? I thought all the kids were playing the bank game."

"No, I said that was too boring, so the nice lady gave me some crayons and let me draw a picture," she replied with a smile, twisting her hips to make her skirt twirl.

"Well, that nice lady certainly doesn't run your meetings like Lane did, now does she?" Campbell looked down at the page and saw the white paper filled with dozens of brightly-colored butterflies. "Look at all of these beautiful butterflies, sweetie!"

The young girl looked up, her Hannigan-blue eyes intense with pride from behind her long, blinking eyelashes. "It's a family of butterflies. Most people won't know that they're a family because they all have different-colored wings, but I know they're a family because they all have the same kind of love in their hearts."

"The same kind of love in their hearts?" Campbell looked away from the page and into her granddaughter's shining face.

Turning to skip away, the young girl yelled over her shoulder, "Yep! Just like us, Mimi! You can keep that one! I'm gonna be making pictures allllll morning!"

"What are you doing out here, slacker? Skipping out on the meeting? You missed out on the financial markets overview, your favorite part." Cole poked his sister in the ribs both literally and figuratively.

"Well, what are you doing out here? You should be in there too!" Campbell retorted with a smile.

"We took a bathroom break. I thought I'd take use the opportunity to call my fiancé." Cole waved his phone, baiting his sister.

"Fiancé?" she asked with a smile.

Cole shook his head shyly. "I asked Brooke to marry me last night, and she said yes!"

Campbell stood up on her tiptoes and threw her arms around her brother. "Congratulations! I'm so happy for you. I just love her. It took you until your sixties, but I'm so glad you've finally found a good woman."

"I'm going to make the announcement to everyone tonight at dinner, but I figured I should tell you individually."

"Well, isn't that thoughtful! You've certainly come a long way, haven't you, Cole Hannigan?"

Cole crossed his arms and dropped his eyes to the ground, processing decades of memories. "I have. I think we all have." Looking up, he motioned his hand toward the children's meeting. "Dad would get a kick out of seeing all of us meeting like this, wouldn't he?" He glanced at his watch and started to walk down the carpeted hallway. "Listen, I've gotta fly. I can't get any reception in the building, and she's expecting my call."

With a full heart, Campbell smiled and finally found peace inside herself.

"Can you see this, Dad?" she spoke with her heart. "In three generations, your Butterfly Trust did just what you hoped it would do—it created all these beautiful butterflies, flying their own bold paths with the same kind of love in their hearts."

YOUR LAST MEETING WITH LANE

1. What vision do you have for how your grandchildren will live their lives or handle wealth?

2. How might you increase the involvement of younger generations in your annual meetings?

3. Would you say that your family members are each "flying their own bold paths with the same kind of love in their hearts"? What causes a family to be unique from one another yet unified in this way? How would you describe the "same kind of love" that your family shares?

4. Now that the story has come to a close, what are the two most important insights you have gained from this book?

5. Share a goal you have set for your own growth as a result of reading this book. Share a hope or dream for your family that formed while you read this book.

6. What first step will you take within the next three days to work toward meeting your goal?

ENDNOTES

Chapter 2
1. Roy Williams and Vic Preisser, *Preparing Heirs: Five Steps to a Successful Transition of Family Wealth and Values*. (San Francisco, CA: Robert D. Reed Publishers, 2003).
2. James E. Hughes Jr. is credited with introducing the various capital areas to the field of legacy planning. His works include *Family Wealth: Keeping It in the Family, Family: The Compact Among Generations*, and *The Voice of the Rising Generation: Family Wealth and Wisdom*. Richard Orlando's book defines the notion of Spiritual Capital, included in Lane's list. *Legacy: The Hidden Keys to Optimizing Your Family Wealth Decisions*. (New Hope, PA; Legacy Capitals Press, 2013).
3. Cary Cherniss and Daniel Goleman, *The Emotionally Intelligent Workplace*. (San Francisco, CA: Jossey-Bass, 2001).

Chapter 3
1. Although the concept had appeared in scholarly journals previously, emotional intelligence was made popular by Daniel Goleman in 1995 with his book *Emotional Intelligence*. There are several EI assessments available. With my coaching clients, I use the SEIP (Social and Emotional Intelligence Profile®) offered through the Institute for Social + Emotional Intelligence®.
2. This quote is from *The Sickness Unto Death*, which Soren Kierkegaard wrote under the pseudonym "Anti-Climacus."

Chapter 5
1. Breton Fisherman's Prayer - This oft-cited prayer is paraphrased in modern day English from a poem by Winfred Ernest Garrison (1874-1969).

Chapter 7
1. James Grubman, *Strangers in Paradise: How Families Adapt to Wealth across Generations*. (Turners Falls, MA: Family Wealth Consulting, 2013).

2. As stated in a previous chapter, this quote is from *The Sickness Unto Death*, which Søren Kierkegaard wrote under the pseudonym "Anti-Climacus."

Chapter 8
1. R. Beckhard and W. Dyer, "Managing Continuity in the Family-Owned Business." *Organizational Dynamics*, 1983, b12, 5-12.

Chapter 9
1. Daniel Goleman, *Emotional Intelligence: Why It Can Matter More Than IQ.* (New York: Bantam Books, 1995). Print.

Chapter 14
1. Og Mandino, *The Greatest Salesman in the World: Featuring the Ten Vows of Success.* (New York, NY: Bantam, 1989).
2. Learn about this research at http://www.adultdevelopmentstudy.org/.

Chapter 15
1. Statistics taken from a survey Financial Advisor Magazine found at www.fa-mag.com/news/article-689.html?print. Other research found that 86 percent of heirs fired their parents' financial advisors after receiving inheritance. Rothstein Kass. "Changing of the Guard." July 2009.

Chapter 16
1. The Holy Bible, New International Version, Matthew 6:19-21.
2. The imagery of the "black hole" that is created by the family business founder or wealth creator's dreams/drive is attributed to Jay Hughes, discussed in his co-authored book, *The Voice of the Rising Generation: Family Wealth and Wisdom.* James E. Hughes, Jr., Susan E. Massenzio, and Keith Whitaker. (John Wiley & Sons, 2014).

Chapter 22
1. Jaffe, Dennis. *Releasing the Potential of the Rising Generation: How Long-Lasting Family Enterprises Prepare Their Successors.* CreateSpace Independent Publishing Platform, 2016. Print

An Ongoing Conversation

If you loved *In Three Generations*,
let's keep the conversation going!
Share reader feedback at coach@inthreegenerations.com

Visit www.inthreegenerations.com for information about:

Upcoming Books, Media, Speaking Engagements

Legacy Coaching/Consulting for your Family

Facilitating a Book Discussion Group
using *In Three Generations*

88164418R00157

Made in the USA
Columbia, SC
01 February 2018